Praise for
Fearless Loving

"The first step to having a loving relationship is to take responsibility for your own emotions, thoughts, and actions. *Fearless Loving* shows you how."
—Michele Weiner-Davis,
author of *The Sex-Starved Marriage* and *Divorce Busting*

"In *Fearless Loving*, Rhonda Britten's 8 Simple Truths deliver her trademark fearbuster exercises in a step-by-step plan any lover can use to review, enhance, and create loving relationships. This book will be a great addition to couples who want to be the best lovers they can be. A must for anyone serious about love." — Lou Paget,
bestselling author of *The Big O*

"Ms. Britten gives the reader thoughtful and creative approaches to conquering fear and doubt in order to love unencumbered. *Fearless Loving* is an enormously helpful book. . . . A guide that is useful, compelling, and, above all, wise."
—Dr. Fred Luskin,
director of the Stanford University Forgiveness Project,
author of *Forgive for Good*

Praise for
Fearless Living

"*Fearless Living* is an inspiring, life-saving book. Rhonda Britten can show you how to leave your fear behind and live your life with freedom and joy. I recommend this book to anyone looking to make his or her life better."
— Dave Pelzer,
New York Times bestselling author of *A Child Called "It"*
and *A Man Named Dave*

"Rhonda Britten has risen from the ashes of genuine catastrophe. She has seen the deepest darkness, and found her way beyond it. Hers was not an easy path, by any means. What she has accomplished...and now helps others to accomplish as well, is nothing short of miraculous."
—Marianne Williamson,
New York Times bestselling author of *A Return to Love* and *Illuminata*

continued . .

CHANGE YOUR LIFE IN
30 Days

A Journey to Finding
Your True Self

RHONDA BRITTEN

A PERIGEE BOOK

A Perigee Book
THE BERKLEY PUBLISHING GROUP
Published by the Penguin Group
Penguin Group (USA) Inc.
375 Hudson Street, New York, New York 10014, USA
Penguin Group (Canada), 10 Alcorn Avenue, Toronto, Ontario M4V 3B2, Canada
(a division of Pearson Penguin Canada Inc.)
Penguin Books Ltd., 80 Strand, London WC2R 0RL, England
Penguin Group Ireland, 25 St. Stephen's Green, Dublin 2, Ireland
(a division of Penguin Books Ltd.)
Penguin Group (Australia), 250 Camberwell Road, Camberwell, Victoria 3124, Australia
(a division of Pearson Australia Group Pty., Ltd.)
Penguin Books India Pvt. Ltd., 11 Community Centre, Panchsheel Park, New Delhi—110 017,
India
Penguin Group (NZ), Cnr. Airborne and Rosedale Roads, Albany, Auckland 1310, New Zealand
(a division of Pearson New Zealand Ltd.)
Penguin Books (South Africa) (Pty.) Ltd., 24 Sturdee Avenue, Rosebank, Johannesburg 2196,
South Africa

Penguin Books Ltd., Registered Offices: 80 Strand, London WC2R 0RL, England

Perigee paperback edition: February 2005
First edition: Dutton 2004

ISBN: 0-399-53069-X

This book has been cataloged by the Library of Congress

PRINTED IN THE UNITED STATES OF AMERICA

10 9 8 7 6 5

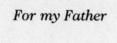

For my Father

Contents

Preface

Whether it is your career or your love life that needs improving, or maybe you just want more self-confidence, the next 30 days have been designed to radically change the way you feel, the thoughts you think, and the things you do.

For twenty years I searched for the true me. I had no idea who I was or what made me feel confused, overwhelmed, or unsatisfied. I constantly thought there must be something wrong with me. There wasn't. I just didn't have the skills to see the truth of who I really was.

Over the next 30 days, I am going to give you the skills you need in order to change your life from the ground up. Because I developed this process through my own healing and have seen millions of people use it to find their true selves, I know this stuff works. What took me twenty years will only take you 30 days if you are willing to focus on one thing a day.

And *focus* is what I had to have in order to change my life. In reality, most people want to alter some aspect of themselves but few are willing to move through the uncomfortable feelings and take the risks necessary to make the changes happen. If you aren't sure you want to change, don't read this book. This book is for those serious seekers who want more out of life.

I had to be serious if I was going to overcome my childhood. I am sure you too have had things happen that have been difficult for you to face. I understand. Yet, your past does not dictate your future. My past was a burden that, at times, seemed too heavy to bear. The blame, guilt, and shame I felt were paralyzing. I just didn't think I was good enough.

Find my true self? I was afraid that that *was* my true self. I am so glad I was wrong.

My most challenging experience that precipitated my desire to change was hard to face as I grew up. My father didn't love me, not the way you'd hope a father would. When I was fourteen years old I looked like I had it all together, but in reality, I wasn't doing so well. My father and mother had recently separated and Father's Day was coming up. I wasn't thrilled to see my dad but I felt obligated. That's when it happened: My father killed my mother and then himself right in front of me. From that day forward, I was frozen in fear that I wasn't good enough. If I had been, wouldn't he have stopped, or at least taken me, too? But there I was, very much alive and very afraid to go on.

I pray that nothing like that has happened to you. Yet, I know we can all relate to one another because we all have feelings. And feelings affect you regardless of how much money you make, your race, religion, or cultural heritage. I have yet to meet a person who has not experienced loneliness, feelings of stupidity, or shame. And not feeling good enough is the common thread that all humans can relate to.

Over the next 30 days, you are going to break down the barriers between success and peace of mind, as well as inner satisfaction and material wealth. Those qualities can all co-exist with each other. The challenge is that you must be willing to do the work when it doesn't seem good or doesn't seem easy.

If you are willing, you will learn that loving yourself has great rewards, and without it, love will feel impossible. You will discover that friends are vital to living without fear, while following your intuition is the pathway to truth.

Many people tell me that my books help them because they are profoundly simple. I don't use fancy words or complicated examples. I don't shame you into changing. I will never berate you or belittle you. Instead, inside these pages you will find the answers to questions that apply to you and your life. Put yourself in the shoes of every example, whether it be about a man or woman. Learn as much as you can from each page. Highlight the important statements and read them over and over. Answer the questions as you go along. Don't be afraid. The answers are here. Let's begin the journey that will change your life.

Day 1

A New Beginning

Congratulations. You have decided to embark on a sacred journey to find your true self. By picking up this book you have committed to making dramatic changes in your life in the next 30 days. I'm asking you to dedicate this month to yourself. This is not a selfish act; on the contrary, as you will learn in this book, it is the most unselfish act you can commit.

I believe that we all secretly yearn to make our lives better while being true to our essential self. To take on this task you might need to learn how to say no, create boundaries, give up people-pleasing, speak up, reignite your passion, find your purpose, let go of false friends and make new ones. Or the task might manifest itself in a more concrete way, like finding a dream job, committing to an exercise program, or falling head over heels in love. For me, being true to myself would include more intangible qualities such as more satisfaction, peace of mind, and self-love. I believe people compromise their dreams too quickly. The truth is you can have it all. You can have the external things you crave while fulfilling your soul's desires if you can answer yes to the following questions:

1. Are you willing to put personal integrity above a promise to another?
2. Are you willing to listen to your heart while using your head?
3. Are you willing to quit lying to yourself in order to start loving yourself?
4. Are you willing to be authentic even if it means being vulnerable?

5. Are you willing to invest in the life you have to get the life you want?

If you answered yes, being true to yourself is a top priority. New beginnings can happen only if you are willing to embrace your true self amid the scars of the past and your hopes for the future, while at the same time being truthful about the life you lead now.

Being true to yourself is not an easy task. What does being true to yourself mean? I think it is the essence of life. What other question wakes you up in the middle of the night, forcing you to examine the areas of your life where you have been lying to yourself or to someone else, and, ultimately, letting your soul down?

Stacey, a thirty-four-year-old antiques dealer, knew she wanted to change her life. Wearing a '50s poodle skirt with her matching shoes and handbag, she could hardly sit still as we spoke about her dilemma.

"The antiques store I manage has been in my family for three generations. My whole family works there. My sister travels all over the country but mainly the Midwest, searching for antiques, my brother heads up the refinishing department, and my job is to make the store profitable. My mother and father still work at the store almost every day, even though I am now in charge of all the operations. They keep talking about retiring, but . . ." Stacey's voice trailed off.

"It sounds like you are close with your family. Is that what you wanted to talk to me about?" I asked.

"Well, yes and no. I want to change my life but I just didn't know where to start. My life is okay but I want more. I want it to be better. I want it to be great," Stacey quickly explained.

I could tell she had high hopes and was praying that I could help her with her goal. I could. But what she didn't realize was she would have to do most of the work. The work started with a simple question.

"Define *great*," I asked.

Defining the words you use supports you in your quest for personal integrity. Do you mean what you say, or say something just for the sake of talking? I am always fascinated when a couple comes into my office to talk about love. Rarely have they defined it for themselves, yet they bat the word around and nod their heads as if they understand each other completely. Not me. I had to know her definition before I could help.

"I had never thought of defining *great* before," she said with an air of uneasiness. She began to fidget with the pen in her hand.

"Defining a word makes it more real," I explained. "It gives the word more weight, more value. If you wanted to have a better life, one that you call 'great,' then you better be willing to define it. So, Stacey, what do you mean by *great*?"

Stacey leaned toward me and began reciting her list of what would make up a great life. "Well, a great life would be taking more time out for me. I would let myself fall in love. I would live in the mountains near a lake. I wouldn't care if I was perfect anymore. I wouldn't think about work every minute of every day. I would relax more and have more fun. I might even get a dog or cat. And I definitely wouldn't care so much about things that didn't matter. Is that what you meant?" she asked.

I smiled. "Yes, that is a good start," I said. "And what I heard you say is that you want more love and fun in your life. Is that right?"

"Yes." Stacey sighed. "It almost seems selfish to want more, but I am just not as happy as I should be. I know I have a great job and good friends, but I am always running around doing things that I don't want to do. Do you know what I mean?"

Oh, yes. I knew what Stacey meant. People who do a lot of things but with little meaning are an epidemic phenomenon nowadays. It has become a world of "should." Most people come to the Fearless Living Institute for that very reason. They may not say it. But that is what they mean. Stacey was going to be all right.

Ask yourself the same question. You are reading this book to change your life in some way, but do you know which way? The more specific you can get, the more likely you will succeed. Being specific is an act of honesty. Can you be specific without allowing social definitions to get in your way?—or in other words, what you think the definition "should" be? When we get caught in the external trappings of success, our internal life will never be satisfied.

I asked Stacey to answer the following questions. If you want to get the most out of this book, answer them for yourself as well.

Being true to yourself would mean:

If you were true to yourself you could:

Be more at peace in myself

If you were true to yourself you would let go of:

Harsh self criticism, need for perfection

For most a better life includes success. To help you determine if success is part of your better or so-called great life, please answer the following:

Define *success:*

rewarding, meaningful purpose - driven life

You felt successful when:

I accomplished difficult tasks, done to my personal level of satisfaction

You would be more successful if:

I could bring my A game all the time.

What would you need to do to have a successful life?

Be better at self - discipline Re: health, appearance + well being choices; + better at accepting my short comings.

What would you have to let go of?

snacking, most junk food, the need to always 'get it right

Knowing what you mean when you describe your "great" life is critical to understanding what you want and, more important, why you get disappointed, stopped, frustrated, and overwhelmed. Why you almost get there but rarely meet the mark. Why your dreams, at times, feel so close yet so far away. Definitions tell you what you believe, who you are, and what you think you are capable of. They indicate whether you trust yourself or are insecure. Do you have faith in what you want or do you waver and write down the safe choice?

Notice how you feel or what you think when you are asked to define a word. Do you want to grab a dictionary to make sure you have the "right" answer? Do you want to poll your friends? Do you go blank? Do you write down the first thing that comes to you? Is it easy or hard? This is valuable to know because it's showing you how you process information. That's important. We will talk more about that later. Just note what you think or feel when you are answering the questions throughout this book.

It always amazes me how one simple question and one simple answer can speak volumes about a person's belief in herself. Look at your answer. Does it put a smile on your face? Do you want to change it? Are you satisfied with your reply? Were you clear and thorough? If someone read your answer, like your fairy godmother, would she know exactly how to make your dreams come true?

Stacey had a hard time separating her family's expectations from her own desires. It had been a given that Stacey would work in the family business ever since she was born. Stacey liked it well enough, but she didn't feel like she ever had a chance to make her own decisions. The traditions handed down from one generation to the next defined her family life and the business. Stacey felt she had no place to be Stacey.

"I know my parents want me to be happy," she explained, "but they also want the store to be my life. I don't think I want the store to be my life. I do want to make them happy, but when is it my turn to make myself happy? To be honest, I don't even know what that would mean. I don't know what to do. It is so confusing."

Stacey was having a difficult time weighing her parents' wants against her own needs, so I decided to shake things up. "Do you want to quit your job?" I asked.

When you answer a question like this, check the authenticity of your reply by asking yourself the following question. I asked Stacey to repeat it until she was sure she was answering the question from her own internal guidance.

Who am I being when I am answering this question?

Stacey answered the question quickly. "No, of course I don't want to quit. I couldn't. It is a family business and I am part of the family." The answer was too pat, too logical, to be from her true self. She realized she was being her mother. "I know my answer was what my mother would say. She has been afraid for years to leave the store. She has told me several times that when she married my dad, she knew she was marrying the store."

When fear is running your life, you will not be true to yourself. It takes vigilance and an honest commitment to move you from the life you have to the life you want. But being true to yourself is the key that will get you there. You must answer every question with the truth. Fear wants our answers to be neat and pretty; freedom doesn't care if the truth is messy.

I asked her again. "Do you want to quit your job?"

"I don't know. It is a great job and I am running a business at thirty-four years old. My parents trust me. Where else could I get a job with so much responsibility that included ownership? And it is a real honor to be part of a tradition like our store has been to so many families for generations."

This time around she found herself putting down the "right" words, the ones that made her feel smart, enlightened, and impressive. She answered it like the perfect daughter. Stacey was an expert at rationalizing.

I asked her again. "Do you want to quit your job?"

"No, not really. But I can't work the way I have been either. I am tired. I want to have a life outside the store, outside my family." Finally, she had found her own answer. It wasn't nice and neat. It was a little bit messy.

A better life for Stacey would include taking time out for herself. Joining a sailing club and not going home for every single birthday and holiday was going to be a start. She wanted to create her own traditions with her group of close-knit friends. She also wanted to wake up happy to be alive.

Seems simple enough, but talking about it and doing it are two different things. What would Stacey have to do to change her life? Leave work early or not come in one or two days a week would be a good place to begin. She could sign up for sailing lessons. What about the holidays? She could tell her family no, and for most folks, especially a family as close as Stacey's, that wouldn't be easy. It might seem silly to want to wake up happy, but it would mean dealing with her problems head-on rather than avoiding them. Simple answers reveal true, deep desires that will fundamentally change your life.

Are you truthful? Are these your dreams of a better life? Is this new life attainable if you are willing to risk everything? If you could have everything you described, would you be happy? Have you earned it? Are you worth it?

Now, think about your answers one more time. This is your final opportunity to determine if this is the life you desire above all else. I will be giving you some key ingredients to activate your answers and turn them into reality.

Is that it?

Fantastic. Thank you for having the courage to face your first difficult task: telling the truth about "great life" and "success." I understand how hard it can be to answer a straightforward question, especially when we have been hurt, disappointed, and frustrated in the past. The fact that you did answer the questions to the best of your ability proves to me you are ready to have a "better" life.

Make sure you get support over the next 30 days. Take a minute to think of a friend or family member who could support you during this journey. Will they tell you the truth? Is he or she a good cheerleader? For instance, are the following words in their vocabulary: "Yes! Go for it! I knew you could do it! You are amazing."

No one can be fearless alone. It takes courage to reach out and ask for help. Do it. It is Day One and it is time for you to take the first step toward finding your true self.

The days ahead will give you the skills and tools to be true to yourself more and more each day. Your future is unfolding already. Get ready for a ride.

Today, Practice Being True to Yourself

Discovering the true you is a journey that begins today. Please answer the following questions and be as thorough and as honest as you can. We have a lot to do in 30 days, so let's get going.

How would being true to yourself change your life?

If you are true to yourself, what are you afraid might happen?

What has stopped you before from becoming the best you possible?

Describe the you that you would like to be in 30 days.

What is one thing you are willing to do today to be more true to yourself?

How you answered the questions above determines your commitment to the journey we are embarking on together. Pay attention to the qualities and characteristics you would like to develop. This will help you decide what area of your life to focus on for the next 30 days.

In order to change your life and claim your best you, I invite you to take the actions necessary to start living the life you described above, including taking the one action today that will help you be more true to yourself. It may be giving up lying for a day or giving up complaining or letting go of a problem that has been nagging you. Your willingness to take this small step determines your ability to fulfill the sacred path you are on to finding the true you.

Today, I want you to remember four points. Think about these four points as you go through the day. These points comprise the first step you will be taking to finding your true self.

1. Defining a word helps to clarify what you believe
2. Being specific with an answer accelerates growth
3. Wanting a better life is really a desire to be more true to yourself
4. Telling the truth is an important part of discovering who you are

$\mathcal{D}ay\ 2$

Give Credit Where
Credit Is Due

As you read the sentence below, what is your immediate response? Go ahead. Take a breath and read the following sentence.

You are doing better than you think you are.

Are you exhilarated? Relieved? Validated? Or maybe you feel misunderstood.

Check the statements that align with your response.

_____ "Rhonda doesn't know me."

_____ "I haven't done enough."

_____ "Thank God someone finally understands me."

_____ "I wish!"

__✗__ "If I am doing better than I think I am, why don't I feel better?"

_____ "I am?!"

_____ "Thank you."

_____ "Don't tell me that! I won't stay motivated."

_____ "You bet I am. I've worked hard."

_____ Other response:_____

Your response to praise tells me how you filter information, and that determines your feelings, thoughts, and behaviors. There are many filters that people use to color the truth. For instance, some people process information through the "I am not good enough" filter while others use the "You couldn't possibly like me" filter. How

you process information creates your perceptions and perceptions create your world.

Let's find out how you think.

If you checked off "Rhonda doesn't know me," you filter other people's words and deeds through "No one knows the real me." If you have friends, they have worked very hard to get close to you. Intimacy isn't your forte. When you do feel connected with another, you have a hard time trusting that they won't go away.

If you checked "I haven't done enough," perfectionism is your filtering system. You pride yourself on working harder and longer than anyone else. Too bad you have little time to take care of you. You are the last person on your list.

"Thank God someone finally understands me" comes from a fear of not being seen. You are seeking validation and seldom feel that people really understand you. If you checked off "I wish!" you filter compliments through the "I know me better than you do" filter. Taking credit is difficult because you don't believe you could ever work hard enough. Deserving success is a major challenge because you focus on what you don't do well rather than what you do well. You have a sense of humor but it rarely makes people genuinely laugh.

If "If I am doing better than I think I am, why don't I feel better?" sounds familiar, your feelings determine your day and override your logic. You have a lot of feelings but hardly any that allow you to feel good about yourself. They can so easily sidetrack you from your goals.

If "I am?!" is your filter, questioning everything others say and do is your mode of operation. Compliments almost never stick because you unconsciously think you don't deserve them. You doubt yourself.

If you accept compliments with a simple thank-you, you have learned that it is important to be gracious when given a compliment. If you believe the compliment regardless of who says it, your self-esteem is high. If you don't believe it, no matter who says it, you have learned the art of "thank you" but you haven't had the confidence to change your life.

"Don't tell me that! I won't stay motivated" is used by folks who beat themselves up and accept negative criticism as fact. Never good enough, they are committed to "fixing" themselves no matter what anyone says. Suffering and struggling are familiar feelings.

The last response listed is "You bet I am. I've worked hard." When you check off that statement, your filtering system includes a healthy dose of self-confidence and a desire to finally give yourself the credit where credit is due. It is important to you to be labeled a success.

Your filtering system may feel real to you, but it is not the truth. As we move through the next few days together, I will be giving you tools to help you alter your perceptions. But before we can change your filter system, it helps to know which particular one yours is. Did you determine your filtering system? What sentence above relates best to how you see the world?

Your filtering system is:

feelings over ride logic

Becoming aware of how your brain interprets events is important if you truly want to change your life in less than 30 days. It's time to get serious about how you think and what you think about.

One way to start shifting your mind-set is to acknowledge all the ways you have stretched. Acknowledgments give you credit and pat you on the back for all of your shifts and changes. Any new thought you think, any new action you take, any new way of being, is an opportunity to stop and praise your willingness to change. It is life changing to acknowledge yourself for every step you take.

Pay attention to the changes you have already made, whether you think they are perfect or not. Sometimes it's risky just "thinking" about a change. This is the time to acknowledge yourself. Trust me, acknowledging yourself will not give you a big head. It will give you the confidence necessary to change your life no matter how you feel, what thoughts you think, or what roadblocks are in your path.

Acknowledgments give you credit for the hard work you are doing. That is vital if you want to fulfill your potential. Don't let your feelings decide if something matters; instead, focus on whether or not you took the action rather than how you felt about it. Your negative feelings will begin to subside when you start acknowledging yourself on a daily basis.

When that happens, your filtering system will naturally change,

allowing a more positive view of the world to come into focus. Your awareness will increase, giving you more insight into who you are, while at the same time building your self-confidence.

Remember Stacey? Her better life included taking the time to sail. She took a risk by calling a local marina and finding out about sailing lessons. For some people it may not sound like a risk, but it was for Stacey. She had been interested in sailing for over ten years but because of her family obligations, she never did anything about it. Making the telephone call brought her one step closer to her dream.

Being as specific as possible, I asked Stacey to complete the following sentence:

Today, I acknowledge myself for _perseverance_ working on tay, clothes, share, health

Stacey wrote: Today, I acknowledge myself for calling a marina and gathering information on the sailing club as well as on how to rent sailboats.

Stacey confided, "I feel so stupid that it took me so long to make a phone call. I am such a loser."

"Believe me, Stacey," I said, "even though you may feel that way, it isn't true. Our judgments about an event stop us from giving credit where credit is due. Just because it was a small step doesn't mean it doesn't have value."

Our fear of failure keeps us from doing the things we yearn to do. Because we do not want to fail. What if Stacey isn't a natural sailor? Does her life become "better" only if she is a perfect sailor? No. It doesn't. Her life becomes better because she took a risk and she is more true to herself because of it.

Go ahead and acknowledge yourself now.

Today, I acknowledge myself for _____.

If you are having difficulty, give yourself credit for buying this book or answering the questions for Day One. For instance:

Today, I acknowledge myself for purchasing *Change Your Life in 30 Days*.
or

Today, I acknowledge myself for reading and completing the exercises up until now.

or

Today, I acknowledge myself for reading today even though I wanted to quit after Day One.

Notice I didn't write down some impossible acknowledgment like: Today, I acknowledge myself for fixing all my problems. That won't change your life. What I did affirm is something that might not seem difficult to others, but is for me. As you read this book you will experience many feelings, including joy and anger. Focus on what you are doing rather than what you are feeling. It will move you one step closer to your better life.

Acknowledging yourself for the risks you are taking in your life will not only begin to change your filtering system but it will also build your self-esteem. Do not focus on whether or not you achieved your ultimate goal. Acknowledgments are about the journey to becoming more true to yourself, not the end result.

Here are some of Stacey's acknowledgments:

Today, I acknowledge myself for exercising again to get in shape for sailing.

Today, I acknowledge myself for being willing to forgive myself for putting myself last.

Today, I acknowledge myself for taking Saturday off to attend sailing class.

Today, I acknowledge myself for telling my parents I am going to start sailing.

Each acknowledgment took courage on Stacey's part. Some took time to accomplish, while others were done quickly. Regardless, each acknowledgment built up her self-esteem.

Let's take the next step. I want you to write down twenty-five acknowledgments for the last year. Acknowledging what you have done in the past will give you more courage to take risks in the present. If the task seems overwhelming, start by focusing on one area of your life at a time. This will support you in being true to yourself.

1. Today, I acknowledge myself for _11,000 steps/day_
2. Today, I acknowledge myself for _"   " " Oct_
3. Today, I acknowledge myself for _"   " " Dec_
4. Today, I acknowledge myself for _"   " " Jan_
5. Today, I acknowledge myself for _"   " " Feb_
6. Today, I acknowledge myself for _"   " " March_
7. Today, I acknowledge myself for _"   " " April_
8. Today, I acknowledge myself for _getting rid of bagel chips_
9. Today, I acknowledge myself for _"   " " choc chips_
10. Today, I acknowledge myself for _re starting stretch tape_
11. Today, I acknowledge myself for _getting chair fixed_
12. Today, I acknowledge myself for _" loungers recovered_
13. Today, I acknowledge myself for _taking bike for repairs_
14. Today, I acknowledge myself for _Annie 40's gifts + party_
15. Today, I acknowledge myself for _great Xmas tree decor_
16. Today, I acknowledge myself for _gingerbread house project_
17. Today, I acknowledge myself for _Danis for T-giving_
18. Today, I acknowledge myself for _lemon tart/pomb w Katie tongs_
19. Today, I acknowledge myself for _pool consultation_
20. Today, I acknowledge myself for _concrete "_.
21. Today, I acknowledge myself for _new glasses_
22. Today, I acknowledge myself for _fixing ceiling hole_
23. Today, I acknowledge myself for _transferring Exxon + Williams Stock_
24. Today, I acknowledge myself for _" Filmo_.
25. Today, I acknowledge myself for _" Sorel_.

Now I want you to do it again. That's right, keep going. You might not think you can do one more acknowledgment for the past twelve months, but you can. Dig deeper. What risks have you taken regarding your job? Did you start a new hobby? Did you speak up to someone whom you had been afraid of in the past? Did you cook a new dish? Did you tell a friend no when you usually say yes? What about taking care of yourself? Did you get a facial for the first time? What about your hair? Did you get a new cut or style? How about your love life? Did you have more compassion? Were you clear on your boundaries? Think about your health. Have you changed anything about your diet? Did you choose your foods more carefully? What about exercise? Hey, if you took one more walk than you did the year before, acknowledge yourself. If you cannot take the time to think this hard about your life, you will never be able to change your life.

26. Today, I acknowledge myself for *getting new HVAC*
27. Today, I acknowledge myself for *helping when I took*
28. Today, I acknowledge myself for *" Annie move. came*
29. Today, I acknowledge myself for *getting appraisals*
30. Today, I acknowledge myself for *" sold "* .
31. Today, I acknowledge myself for *Mom Dad's funeral*
32. Today, I acknowledge myself for *filing 706 form*
33. Today, I acknowledge myself for *completing taxes 2018*
34. Today, I acknowledge myself for *shopping for luggage*
35. Today, I acknowledge myself for *trip to Oxford* .
36. Today, I acknowledge myself for *tickets to London*
37. Today, I acknowledge myself for *train tickets Scotland*
38. Today, I acknowledge myself for *blueberry pie at Mar ma's*
39. Today, I acknowledge myself for *quit-claim Nebr.*
40. Today, I acknowledge myself for *Ia. farm lease, etc.*
41. Today, I acknowledge myself for *Moms trust & taxes*
42. Today, I acknowledge myself for *2 Breast Exams*
43. Today, I acknowledge myself for *great Xmas gifts brands*
44. Today, I acknowledge myself for *trip to Tahoe*
45. Today, I acknowledge myself for *trip to C. Richardson*
46. Today, I acknowledge myself for *Costa noca RSVP*
47. Today, I acknowledge myself for *V & A tickets* .
48. Today, I acknowledge myself for *monthly facials*
49. Today, I acknowledge myself for *wearing make-up*
50. Today, I acknowledge myself for *purging lots* .

You did it! Great work!

Go ahead and look at all of your acknowledgments. To accomplish each one, you had to face a fear in order to take the risk. With every acknowledgment you are getting closer to the true you. Congratulations. You are changing your life.

Today, Acknowledge Yourself

Take a few moments and answer the following questions. They will help you focus on what is important today.

In what area of your life do you have a hard time giving yourself credit? *all areas*

In what area would you like to acknowledge yourself more?
all areas

What could happen if you gave yourself more credit?
I would feel better about myself + actions

Are you willing to give yourself more credit?
It is 1 of my goals for 2019. Will try harder to do this

Please write down five acknowledgments every day for the next thirty days, starting now. Focus on what risks you took today. Again, think small. Be specific. You are learning to be aware of all the good things you do on any given day. This allows you to grow confident in yourself. And reveals, slowly at first, who your true self actually is. The smaller and more specific, the better.

1. Today, I acknowledge myself for _____.
2. Today, I acknowledge myself for _____.
3. Today, I acknowledge myself for _____.
4. Today, I acknowledge myself for _____.
5. Today, I acknowledge myself for _____.

Focus on where and when it is easy to acknowledge yourself while at the same time noticing where you are stingy with credit. Learning to focus on what you are doing, versus what you want to do, will help you stay true to yourself moment by moment.

Day 3

Building Your
Confidence Muscle

Take a few moments to answer the questions and fill in the
blanks. There are no wrong answers. Write down the first
thought that comes to your mind.

Define *confidence:*

*belief in one's self — the ability to do what set
out to do*

How would you know if you had confidence?

*you feel a comfortable sense of security —
"I've got this"*

I want to build my confidence in the area of *self discipline to*
If I had more confidence I could *be there & stay there.* *promote health*
When I am with a confident person I feel *safe or challenged* *wellness*
When I feel confident I can *get it done*.
I am confident *80 - 90* percent of the time.
If I had more confidence, I would be truer to myself because

_____.

Self-confidence is the result of taking risks. Once you have successfully taken risks, you have learned through your experiences
that you can count on yourself. Your belief that you can accomplish

something risky is based in truth. There is no ego involved. You are willing to take on challenges and are always doing the best you can.

Confidence is something everyone wants but few are willing to do the work to achieve. Being willing to feel your feelings and face your fears are two of the risks you must be willing to take in order to gain confidence. The good news is anyone can have more confidence. It is a function of consistent effort, compassion, and willingness.

You may not think confidence has anything to do with compassion, but it does. Most of us are so hard on ourselves, we won't make the effort that is necessary to achieve long-lasting results if it includes feeling stupid, silly, or inadequate. Any risk you take may make you feel any or all of those things. In order to gain confidence you must be willing to feel every feeling and take actions regardless of those same feelings.

"Rhonda, if I only had more confidence, I would have the courage to be true to myself and get my dream job (marry the girl, lose weight, fall in love, let go of guilt, learn to say no, find my purpose, etc.)."

I can't tell you how many times people tell me, "If only I had confidence, THEN I could change my life." But confidence doesn't come first. Risk does.

In order to gain confidence you must take the risk you do not want to take. Confidence does not happen once in your life and then you have it for good. Confidence must be exercised just like any other muscle on your body. Confidence must be nurtured in order for it to grow.

That is the secret to building your confidence. You must take risks in order to learn how to count on yourself, which in turn creates confidence. The feelings you experience can be extremely uncomfortable. Fear tells us that no risk is worth it. Yet, learning to be comfortable being uncomfortable while feeling your feelings and taking risks is an important ingredient in being true to yourself.

You can't wait for confidence to happen, first you must go for it and then confidence is the result. Therefore, the only way you will build confidence is to do the thing you fear.

I understand that taking risks and feeling uncomfortable is not the most pleasant experience, yet nothing will give you so much personal satisfaction. During our journey together, you will have numerous opportunities to stretch your view of who you are and what you are capable of. You will learn that you are more valuable than you know. This will help you claim it.

When I hear the word *confidence* it immediately brings to mind the ups and downs I have experienced while healing my past. I had broken more promises to myself than I can remember. It was promise, fail, promise, fail, promise, fail. If I told myself I was going to go to the gym three times this week, I can guarantee you it didn't happen.

Being able to count on yourself to do your best is an important aspect of confidence. Another trait of confident people is they aren't afraid of looking stupid, silly, or foolish.

This is one I learned for myself. I am frequently asked how I learned to give talks that inspire and change lives. My answer is always the same: I quit caring about being perfect and just spoke from my heart. Until I was willing to take a risk and look foolish, I looked like a robot as I spoke showing little emotion. It was horrible. I had to give up becoming the perfect speaker to become the best speaker I could be. I had to risk feeling uncomfortable to build true confidence.

Some people determine confidence by outside appearances or how someone articulates or how much money they have in the bank. All of those things build external confidence, yet they have nothing to do with internal confidence. Your internal confidence determines your ability to accept compliments, go for the job promotion, or ask the person you are attracted to out on a date. The confidence that exists on the inside will support you for years to come.

External success does not guarantee confidence. I have met many people who do extremely well in business but are incapable of being true to who they are. They have lied their way to the top and confidence is nowhere to be seen. Kirk was one of my clients who wanted to change his life after he realized earning a million a year wasn't making him happy or giving him the courage he needed to be true to himself.

Kirk was an inventor and a successful one at that. He created some of the household gadgets you have in your house today and now hires other inventors to develop award-winning products. It took great courage for him to trust his instincts when he started to create products, but he hadn't learned how to apply this same courage to other parts of his life.

I asked Kirk to create a list of moments in his life when he felt confident. I didn't ask for a list of events that turned out well. I wanted to know about the times he was vulnerable yet felt strong. Go ahead and make the same list. Give me your top ten confident moments.

1.
2.
3.
4.
5.
6.
7.
8.
9.
10.

Kirk's list included:

1. Watching his only child be born
2. Earning his first paycheck when he was fourteen years old for delivering papers
3. Driving across the country when he was eighteen
4. His wedding day with Jane
5. Being able to afford his first full set of pots and pans when his wife, Jane, was pregnant
6. Hiring the first inventor for his company
7. Finishing his first article for a magazine
8. His third date after his divorce from Jane when he realized he was going to be okay
9. Learning to play the guitar
10. Hiking in New Zealand by himself after his divorce

With such a wide and varied list I was touched by how he included them as confidence boosters. I knew I could take that vivid memory and help him create a new life for himself. But first he had to give up his false confidence and replace it with a true sense of himself.

What do you think of your confidence top ten list? Are the items work related? Love related? What is the common theme? For Kirk his common theme was firsts. When it was the second time around, he didn't give himself credit and his confidence dropped.

It amazes me how we stop ourselves from being true to ourselves because we don't believe we have the confidence to push past our fear of being judged. That is the irony: In order to be confident you must be willing to experience the fears you have been trying to hide from, like your fear of rejection or loss.

Kirk realized that he would keep the same job if he was confident but just enjoy it more and not work so hard. But the surprise for him was in the friendship department. Kirk discovered that if he was truly confident, he wouldn't hang around with his so-called friends.

"I guess I shouldn't be surprised," said Kirk. "I always brag about how my friends really like me, but I guess I forget to mention that I don't really like them."

It was clear that his friendships were intact because he thought he needed them but didn't necessarily want them. Big difference. Do you need and/or want your friendships? Be honest with yourself. As I help you change your life, friendships are critical to support your future growth and transformation past these initial 30 days.

To help Kirk come up with solutions to his friend problem he had some excavating to do.

Name three challenges you are facing right now. Perhaps you are feeling guilty or frustrated about an event in your life. List them now:

1. *physical well being / fitness / health*
2. *connections*
3.

Now, imagine that you had confidence. What would you do differently?

1. *spend time outdoors, do challenging physical*
2. *activities — Half dome vc*
3. *reach out to people I who i admire*
   expect more help making life rewarding

What feelings are you afraid to feel regarding these circumstances?

1. *fear of illness, vomiting, major head-*
2. *ache pain or other physical pain*
3. *~~ineptness~~ — ineptness*
   vulnerable, w/o control

If you were no longer afraid of your feelings and could count on yourself, what could be the happy ending for these challenges?

1. *healthy, fit, doing physically demanding things*
2. *wide network of friends, relationships w*
3. *people I liked, loved, admired*
rewarding, fun life

What could you gain or learn from these situations that you can apply to other areas of your life?

1. *confidence, support, skills,*
2.
3.

What is keeping you from getting that result?

1. *fear of risking*
2.
3.

Learning to identify how confidence helps, and the lack of it hinders, your ability to be true to yourself is crucial in gaining the courage to take more risks. In order to make radical changes in your life, risk and confidence are two key components for your success.

Feelings can get in the way of the truth. So please acknowledge yourself daily. Eventually your feelings and the truth will become more aligned. When you are willing to see the truth instead of acting on just your feelings, you will clear your filtering system of misperceptions. The willingness to learn something from every single situation regardless of your confidence level will also help you identify what is standing in your way.

Confidence does help us bring about the results we desire, in granting us the ability to ask for what we want, express our opinion, and follow through. Those skills are clues that confidence is present.

After Kirk completed the exercise, he knew what he needed to do.

"I have this little condominium in my hometown of Minneapolis. I think I need to spend a little time back home and rediscover what true friendship is all about. My best friend from high school is still living there and I hate to admit it, but I think that is the last person I was with that I was really myself, no masks, just me," said Kirk.

Kirk was willing to give up all he had in order to be true to himself. That is another sign that confidence exists. You must be willing to throw it all away to find your true self. I am not saying you will literally have to give it all away, but you must be willing to risk it, at least metaphorically. Once you do that, you will gain the confidence and the courage to know what to keep and what to leave behind. Be ready for anything.

Today, Build Your Confidence

List ten confident moments that you had today. I understand your confidence may have waned, but reminding yourself you were confident at one moment during that encounter will help you focus on what matters.

Confident Moments:

1. *letting go of harsh self judgement*
2.
3.
4.
5.
6.
7.
8.
9.
10.

Your willingness to give yourself credit is an important step in building confidence. Be sure to complete your five acknowledgments today. Acknowledgments help you stay focused on what is working in your life, and that nurtures confidence. Keep growing.

What decision has been avoided because you haven't had the confidence to decide?

Name one thing that you would do right now if you had more confidence.

Would you be able to make more money? How much more?

If you were confident, would you have the same job? Friends? Mate?

You can watch yourself become more confident. It is incredibly exciting to experience yourself growing confident. The reason I want you to address the issue of confidence early in your 30 days is because as you get closer to changing your life, the more and more confident you will become. It is one of the most important early steps in the journey. Here are five clues that your confidence is growing:

1. You can count on yourself. You do what you say and get the job done.
2. You are willing to feel your feelings and take a risk anyway. No matter how scary things get, you always remember that feelings do not determine success, risk does!
3. Facing your fears is a daily experience. See fear for what it is: an affirmation of your growth.
4. You have learned to be comfortable in the uncomfortableness of change. You have put your negative voice in perspective and realize it does not run your life.
5. You are willing to give up all you know to discover your true you. You have given up justifying your actions; instead, your life speaks for itself. Your main commitment is to keep growing, and therefore you have let go of your need to always be right.

Court your confidence. Take risks daily. Acknowledge your growth. Stand in the awareness that good things are happening in your life because of you, not despite you. Claim confidence as your birthright, and being true to yourself will become easier than you ever imagined.

Day 4

Purpose and Passion

I had just finished a speech at a *Fortune* 500 company when Joan pulled me aside. She was concerned about her job. Yes, she explained, she did love what she was doing and she did respect the people she worked with, but she was afraid it wasn't her true purpose.

"My coworker Samantha told me that she likes her job but her true purpose is working with Habitat for Humanity. She spends every weekend building houses and loves it. And Carl, a really good friend of mine, quit his job yesterday in order to pursue his newfound passion, becoming a massage therapist. I didn't really think about purpose before, but now I can't quit asking myself, What is my purpose? I don't want to waste my life."

Joan could hardly contain her excitement as this latest insight bubbled out of her. It was evident to me she wanted to know her purpose and she wanted to know it NOW!

I think that we believe a purpose will give our lives meaning, will make us feel special and more important, will give us permission to express our hidden passion. We all have passion, but most people are afraid of it. Sure, they want to feel more alive, but at what expense? Passion and purpose are so misunderstood. And in order to change your life in 30 days they must be harnessed and accessed like never before.

What exactly is purpose and passion? When we have a sense of purpose, we become focused and determined. We are single minded. Purpose may stem from a childhood hobby or a social injustice. Academy Award–winning director Steven Spielberg started making movies when he was a child. Martin Luther King, Jr., wanted to right a social injustice and prove that all men are created equal. Purpose may come from a personal experience, as did Mothers Against Drunk Driving (MADD). It was formed in 1980 when thirteen-year-old Cari Lightner was killed by a drunk driver. Her mother, Candy, joined with other women who had lost loved ones and created MADD. Driven by a purpose, MADD is now the largest crime victims' assistance organization in the world.

Rob Bockstruck, a jeweler in St. Paul, Minnesota, inherited his purpose. Bockstruck Jewelers had been around for decades, yet after graduating from college Rob didn't want anything to do with the family business. One year later he was back. Why? He tried to run away from his legacy but as he got farther away he realized that he did love jewelry, not for any other reason than it gave him pleasure. He has since increased the family business because he accepted his purpose.

So you see, purpose can be found in the most unexpected places. Your purpose could be feeding the hungry or creating new, environmentally safe products or something as simple as being a loving person. The myth of purpose is that it has to be grand. Many of the most memorable people started out with no fanfare, no big purpose. Take Abraham Lincoln. He didn't set out to change the world. He only wanted to do the right thing in a time when the right thing wasn't easy to discern. Mother Teresa took care of the starving people on the streets of Calcutta. Neither of their missions were glamorous, but they were driven by purpose just the same.

Many people tell me they want to find their purpose. I always say the same thing: It's right in front of you. Purpose already exists. You must be willing to see it. For instance, do you have something you love to do but don't think you can make money doing it? Is there something that you do that comes so easily to you, that you don't think it could possibly be your purpose? Do you enjoy creating or expressing yourself in a particular area but don't feel it is a big enough purpose?

Passion is the spark, the motivation, the drive, behind a purpose. Passion takes away the sense of obligation a purpose can imply and instills a sense of play and fun. Actress Bette Midler is passionate. No matter what she does she gives a hundred percent of herself, whether it is performing on Broadway or planting a garden in the inner city or producing a movie. She is fully present, awake, and alive. That is passion. Same goes for Sting, a musician superstar, who gives of himself while writing a song, enjoying his family, or raising money to save the rainforest through his Rainforest Foundation.

Passion and purpose are interconnected as well as being integral components of happiness. Having a purpose allows us to express our passion, and if we are passionate, purpose comes alive through our interactions with others. Without them we are disconnected, lost, and our lives can feel meaningless.

When people tell me they want to achieve a goal, they are either looking for the passion to achieve it or the purpose to believe in it. Picture a car. You need fuel to go anywhere (passion) and you need a key to start the motor (purpose). Now you are in the driver's seat and you can either use these tools constructively or destructively. It is up to you.

Purpose directs passion and passion ignites purpose. Without a clear purpose our passion is easily misdirected. Addictions, many times, are passion gone awry. Without passion we might be able to see where we want to go but we don't have the motivation to get there. Purpose is waylaid.

Look at your life. Do you have passion? Do you have enough fuel to change your life? And do you have a purpose? Do you have the key that will allow your passion to be ignited? That is the dance of passion and purpose. They are two heads of the same coin. One cannot live fully and completely without the other.

Let's begin our quest for a purpose that will uncover who we are meant to be and give us the permission to live the life of our dreams. Let's look at the areas where you may or may not have passion and purpose.

Love and career are the two areas most people want to change, because, I suspect, they are the two areas that lack passion. And the two areas in which, if we felt the passion, we would allow ourselves to be overtaken by it. We would say we couldn't stop ourselves or it must be our "destiny." We are hesitant to believe we are in charge of our passion, but we are.

I wonder how many marriages could be saved if each spouse took responsibility for the passion in their love life. How many careers could be rekindled if passion wasn't something to fear but something to cultivate.

We say we want passion and purpose but we avoid it like the

plague. I think we are afraid. Afraid of passion. Afraid of purpose. Afraid of the power we feel when we experience a passion that overwhelms us and a purpose that pushes us to take risks. It seems too scary, too big, and too much. It puts our safe, controlled lives on notice. You can't be safe and be passionate at the same time. Passion takes courage, and purpose asks us to be true to ourselves at all costs. But we hesitate, because fear thrives on safety.

Having passion in our lives does not mean letting it all go and just having fun. Passion is a powerful feeling that is a true confidence builder. It must be nurtured. Passion is power and one must be responsible for it. But most people do not equate passion and responsibility. The misunderstanding causes the passionate person to be labeled wild or irresponsible, while the purpose-driven can be seen as insensitive, selfish, or controlling.

I believe our quest for our soul mate and our perfect career is really a calling for more passion in our lives. Let's face it, who can stop a man in love or a women with a mission? No one. They are unstoppable. Why? Because they possess undeniable drive, focus, and clarity.

The two areas of our lives call for a commitment to be passionate in pursuit of a purpose-driven career and finding the love of all loves, a soul mate. When people ask me to help them find their purpose, they are asking me to help them recapture their passion.

How does passion show up in your life right now?

What would your friends say about you if you were more passionate? Coworkers? Family?

What is scary about passion?

Name three things that you fear would happen if you were more passionate.

Name three things that could occur that would change your life if you were more passionate.

Giving yourself kudos for the passion you give yourself permission to display is essential if you desire to express and experience more passion. One way to identify the fears that squelch your passion is to ask yourself what you think others would say if you were the passionate person you want to be. Even though we would like to think of ourselves as self-reliant, we rarely ignore our negative self-talk generated by our fears of what our friends would think. That can stop us from doing almost anything in our life.

To support you in moving through the fear, focus on the freedom you would gain if you did express your passion. Naming the things that might change gives you a heads-up in preparing for potential fear-inducing roadblocks.

It's time to expand your definition of passion. To rekindle and redefine passion, please list twenty-five things you love. It could be that you get great pleasure from pruning rosebushes or drinking an incredible cup of coffee. Listing your loves will help you reconnect to the things that support your feeling passion in your life. Please write down everything you love, no matter how silly or embarrassed you might be.

1. My family- kids
2. grance
3. Dee - D.S, S
4. coffee + lattes
5. out doors in peaceful quiet especially
6. new places + experiences

7. *good books*
8. *wine (and snacks)*
9. *cool shoes / outfits*
10. *journaling*
11. *feeling well — little pain*
12. *history*
13. *kindness*
14. *democracy /civic life*
15. *art*
16. *beauty — in nature, design, products*
17. *comfort*
18.
19.
20.
21.
22.
23.
24.
25.

Loving people, places, things, events, situations, animals, etc., helps you connect to the world and to your passion about life. When we look for the love in every moment, we are expanding our world instead of making it smaller. We are connecting. We are one with life. We are passionate.

When you heed the calling of your heart, you are following your purpose. Having purpose in your life gives you the courage to do the things you are meant to do. When you are purpose driven, you have learned to listen to your intuition and never let *no* get in your way. Some people think it is selfish to be motivated and inspired in all that they do. True purpose is never selfish. It is impossible for it to be so. Purpose that is coming forth from your true self is always expressed for the good of mankind. It may look like you are just bagging groceries, but you know your purpose is to send love to every customer. Purpose transcends job titles.

Joan realized that she loved supporting people when they were changing their lives. "I never realized before that what is similar in all the things I love is a commitment to growth. Whether I am gardening or talking to a friend on the phone, it only interests me if things are changing. I don't like things to stay the same. I used to think that was a weakness, but maybe it isn't. Maybe it has something to do with my purpose."

"The quest for your purpose is an innate desire to fulfill your destiny, fulfill your potential," I told Joan. "Knowing you are naturally curious about change is a great insight. Now it is time to keep track of the activities you do in your everyday life that may give you a clue as to how your purpose will unfold."

I asked Joan to keep a list of all the times she felt she was supporting change in a person or situation. This would help her to realize when she is already living her purpose as well as to discover the areas where her skills could be developed.

"I got it," she exclaimed as she walked into my office. "I want to be a Life Coach just like you. I realized that I love nothing more than our sessions together. And when I looked at my life, I noticed I get passionate whenever anybody approaches me for help. I think I've found my purpose."

It is exciting when your purpose clicks into place, yet I cautioned Joan to pay attention to what she liked to do rather than how she was going to do it. If Joan feels her purpose is to guide others, she can do it as a Sunday School teacher, being a Little League coach, or becoming a mentor for an organization like Big Sister. Being a Life Coach isn't the answer. It's a choice.

Invest in the life you have to get the life you want.

I told Joan it was time to invest fully in the life she had now. You do the same. Consider it your purpose. Folks get upset when I tell them that, but it is true. When you invest in the life you have, you learn to be fully satisfied where you are right now. Being open to the lessons learned and the tools provided, you will begin to see purpose in every moment rather than in a specific career. It seems simple, but it is very difficult to do because you must let go of everything you know. You must let go of perceptions of who you think you are to find out the truth.

When we practice being true to ourselves, we are given opportunities that we could never have imagined. Focus on expressing your true nature through your passionate purpose and endless gifts will be given to you.

That is what happened to me. I was just trying to heal myself when I developed Fearless Living. I didn't plan on it. It was an accident that happened while I was working on being me. True satisfaction comes from knowing that all you do makes a difference and nothing you do makes a difference. When you find your purpose, results suddenly don't matter as much but you complete all your tasks whether it gets you anywhere or not. Because you must.

When you take the time to embrace the lessons you have learned, you are opening yourself up to the purpose hidden within. Everyday lessons can point you to your purpose. Our purpose defines us, and our ability to express our passion equates with our ability to let go and trust. For some it includes a connection to something larger than us. It could be called God, Buddha, Messiah, Universal Light, and so on. Our greatest human need is to feel connected, to belong. Our ability to claim our purpose and express our passion ensures we won't feel alone ever again.

You are already living your purpose. It is right in front of you. The job you have right now is part of your purpose. The people you encounter are helping you fulfill your purpose. The home you live in supports your purpose. Purpose isn't magical or miraculous. Purpose unfolds as you take the day you are given and practice being more loving, more compassionate, more grateful. Allow passion to inspire you and purpose to guide you, and your life will change for the better.

Today, Focus on Passionate Purpose

Passion and purpose are often the reasons someone wants to change his or her life for the better. You need to know what they are. Answer the questions below.

What is your purpose?

Name three lessons you can learn from your present living situation.

self reliance, resilience

Name three lessons you can learn from your present job.

Name three lessons you can learn from your present relationships.

Skills - computer, Cooking, shopping,
Fun
loving to grief / Sadness

Understanding the lessons within your experiences will help you find the purpose behind all you do. Pay attention to how much passion you allow into your life today. Today is the day for you to begin to see passion and purpose as your birthright. Claim them. Express them. Appreciate the moments they present.

Today, focus on how you feel when you are experiencing passion either in yourself or another. Fulfill your purpose today by learning the lessons in front of you and practicing expressing your true nature.

As you go through your day, think about how passion and purpose can be integrated into your life. Always remember:

- Your purpose is already within you
- Passion gives you the desire to succeed
- Passion without purpose can be perceived as being unfocused and confused
- Purpose without passion can make life feel like a chore

Day 5

Affirmations, Intentions, and Goals

It's time to dissect the difference among affirmations, intentions, and goals. You have heard all the self-help gurus talk about writing down your goals for guaranteed success. While I believe that is a fine exercise to do, it's just half of the recipe. Without all of the ingredients you might manifest a form of outer success, but you will never achieve inner satisfaction.

I have met few people who are willing to accept only material success. Sure, we crave it at the start of our journey. Who doesn't want to live well? But living well is different from being happy. Living well might include buying a new car every year, a big five-bedroom house on the beach, and exotic vacations, but it doesn't guarantee happiness. I wonder how successful you have been balancing your drive for material goods with your desire for inner peace.

What I am about to share with you will help you do both. I am going to show you how inner satisfaction and outer success do not have to be mutually exclusive.

Once again, writing down goals is a good idea, yet without putting them in proper context, goals can seem scattered, unrelated. That is about to change.

When you think in terms of affirmations, intentions, and goals, your desires will start to feel more attainable and your confidence will rise. Let me explain the difference among affirmations, intentions, and goals and then how putting them all together can create synergy that will propel you to make the changes you desire.

Kerry wanted to fall in love. Her friend, Debbie, told her about affirmations. Affirmations are written as if the desired result is happening right now, using positive words in the present tense. The theory is that these statements help focus you, thereby creating a force field that will draw the desired result into your life. For Kerry this meant drawing in the love of her life.

Kerry decided to give it a try. Nothing else was working, so she sat down and created an affirmation that she was supposed to repeat ten times a day without fail.

Kerry's affirmation: "I am now in a loving relationship."

Kerry had been saying her affirmation an average of ten times a day for the past 30 days while looking into a mirror, gazing into her own eyes. Watching yourself speak affirmations is supposed to heighten your connection to the words, giving the affirmation more oomph. She was feeling hopeful that it was working. She knew she wasn't in a loving relationship, but she was willing to try anything to bring love into her life. And tonight was the big singles party. There were going to be hundreds of available men there. She could barely wait.

While she was getting dressed for the event that evening, she kept repeating her affirmation over and over again. "I am now in a loving relationship. I am now in a loving relationship. I am now in a loving relationship." Tonight was the night. After all, she had been doing her affirmations faithfully and was feeling a tad more confident, even though her negative voice would chime in, No, you're not, when she'd finish repeating her affirmation. But Kerry knew she couldn't wait to make her negative voice go away.

Now, there is nothing wrong with affirmations if they empower, motivate, and inspire you. I have used them occasionally to help keep me centered. When I want to reconnect to some accomplishment I have done in the past, I will use an affirmation to boost me up. For instance, I know I am an excellent public speaker. You learned in Day Two that there is nothing arrogant about a statement like this. In fact, it's healthy to be able to say or write down statements such as this one. I get rave reviews after every speech, standing ovations are a regular occurrence, and companies ask me back time and time again. But let's say I am having a day where nothing is going right. I might say to myself, "I am an excellent public speaker and this speech will change lives." This will help me focus on what I want—giving a great speech—rather than what I don't want—a reminder of my bad day.

Kerry used hers to help her focus too. She walked into the party whispering the affirmation under her breath: "I am now in a loving relationship." Each man she met, she imagined that he was The One. At the end of the night, no closer to finding Mr. Right than before the party, Kerry felt useless. She thought, I can't even make an affirmation work.

The next morning she called her friend Debbie and cried, mumbling something about tweaking her affirmation. She must be doing it wrong. Perhaps she had forgotten something. She felt so stupid. Debbie assured her she was doing it properly but maybe, she suggested, Kerry should add the word *intimate* to her affirmation. Aha, thought Kerry. That's it. And off she went repeating her new affirmation, "I am now in a loving intimate relationship," convinced that this time it would work. But it didn't. It just made Kerry feel guilty and ashamed about being Kerry. Three months later Kerry is still single and thinks she is a loser when it comes to affirmations.

Kerry's affirmation didn't make her feel good, it made her feel bad, because every time she said, "I am now in a loving relationship," the voice of fear inside her head would say, No, you're not. She hated it. Also, Kerry's affirmation gave her no guidance on how to change her behavior. It forced her to focus outside of herself to get her result. Every man she would meet who didn't turn into Mr. Right was deciding if her affirmation was succeeding rather than her.

That is when Kerry made an appointment to solve her love crisis. It is challenging to make the changes we need without support when our confidence is low. Kerry needed a coach to help guide her. I began by telling her about intentions.

An intention is a proactive statement written in the present tense that encompasses an overall attitude toward life. Your intention will supersede any one goal. An intention will help you, immediately, feel more empowered because you are responsible for its success. The result will be determined by you, not by anyone else. It will increase your sense of personal power and ability to make things happen. An intention statement includes one critical twist: It has to be written in such way as to inspire you to *do* something.

Kerry still had the same desire: She wanted to be in a loving relationship. That was fine. But where she was off was when her self-esteem was being decided by whether her affirmation came to fruition or not.

She had to wait for something to happen *to* her rather than activate change from within. Intentions are purpose-driven, overarching statements that put you in charge.

I asked Kerry to create an intention statement that would focus her on what she wanted—a relationship—and that included something she could control. She was having a difficult time coming up with a perfect one.

"Kerry," I asked, "how do you want to be in your future relationships?"

She quickly answered. "To be more loving, of course. I want to practice being more loving. I get too impatient and want things now. I focus on how every guy isn't right for me instead of looking at what they do have. I cut men out of my life before they have a chance."

"And what about loving yourself?" I asked.

"Yes," she answered, "I could get better at that as well."

"You did it. You just created your intention. It is something you can *do* that is written in the positive, in the present tense, with ultimate responsibility for its success on you. And the bonus: It is an intention that could last a lifetime."

Kerry was barely able to hold back her excitement. "What do you mean? I didn't write one yet."

"You may not have written it down, but you just said it," I assured her. "I heard, 'I am now loving in all of my relationships.' Does it fit the requirements of an intention statement?"

Kerry checked her list to make sure the intention had everything it needed in order to assure success. Framed in positive? Check. Focused on what I want? Check. Present tense? Check. I am responsible for its success? Check. Bigger than any one goal? Check. It inspires me to *do* something? Check.

"It fits," cried Kerry. "And it doesn't make me feel guilty or ashamed. 'I am now loving in all my relationships.' Now I need help figuring out some of the actions I could take."

That's where goals come in. Goals support your intention. If you concentrate on goals alone, it will not be satisfying because the goal will not be connected to the big picture. Having an intention statement and then achieving the goal will help you succeed in putting your priorities in order.

Kerry's intention statement: "I am now loving in all my relationships." It put Kerry in charge of her destiny.

I asked Kerry, if she practiced being more loving, would she have more love in her life? Her answer was an unequivocal yes. "And if you were more loving, do you think you would find the love of your life with more ease and less stress?" Again, her answer was yes.

Now it was time to create some goals to support her newfound intention. Depending on how she wanted to practice being more loving, her goals would vary from something as simple as smiling at five strangers a day (to up the ante she could add "attractive men" to her goal) to something more challenging, asking three men out in the next forty-eight hours.

Goals can either be daily goals, time-dependent goals, or long-term goals. For instance, Kerry wants to fall in love. A daily goal could include doing something loving for herself while a long-term goal could be saving some money for the vacation of her dreams. Smiling at five attractive men a day could be a daily goal until Kerry becomes more comfortable around men. At that time she would switch her daily goal to keep risking.

Affirmations are positive, result-oriented statements written in the present tense. Kerry's affirmation: I am now in a loving relationship.

Intentions are positive statements written in the present tense that inspire you to create and complete proactive behaviors.

Kerry's intention: I am now loving in all my relationships.

Notice that Kerry's intention is bigger than any one relationship. It includes all of her encounters; therefore, she can practice various ways to love in all different types of relationships. She can practice her intention with family, friends, dates, coworkers, and even strangers. Remember, your intention statement will help you be a better person with everyone you meet, not just one specific person in your life.

Goals support an intention. They are also flexible, because they can be changed, altered, or adjusted. They are things you do, actions you take. Goals can be created for specific situations. The more varied your goals, the more you are able to practice your intention in any situation.

Kerry's goals: Make small talk with one stranger a day. Learn how to flirt. Have a party at my home and ask my friends to invite their friends.

When Kerry started to live through her intention, intimacy was easier to create with her family and friends. Her relationships deepened and she felt more connected to the people she loved. It was then that love found her.

Kerry was getting into the elevator of her apartment complex when a new neighbor walked in. His name was Brian. She'd never seen him before but at six feet two with green eyes smiling at her, she liked what she saw. Kerry decided she was going to practice her intention.

She wasn't going to let a casual elevator ride stop her from connecting. With her new confidence she began to chitchat, asking him questions about where he was from and what he liked to do. She found out he was new in the area and worked in sales. Before you know it the elevator door was opening, and it was her turn to get out. Kerry turned to him one last time and said, "If you need help learning the neighborhood, stop by. I live in 5102. Oh, and my name is Kerry."

He thanked her for the offer. After the elevator door slammed shut behind her, Kerry jumped up and down. She could barely contain her excitement when she called my office.

"Rhonda, you can't believe it. I just met a guy and I didn't wait for him to go first. I started the conversation. I am so proud of myself. Can you believe it?" Kerry was talking so fast, I could barely keep up.

I could believe it. And Kerry and Brian have been dating for over three months. Just a few months ago this conversation would have been impossible for her. Nerves would have kept her quiet. She would have missed Brian. Imagine. Their relationship started all because she focused on her intention to be more loving. Intentions are powerful statements that can make dreams come true. Focus on how you want to change in your life and watch miracles happen.

Today, Live with Intention

I want you to determine how one of your desires could be turned into an affirmation, an intention, and broken down into goals.

Think of a result you want in a specific area of your life. Now claim that you have achieved it by stating it in the present.

My affirmation:

I am happy living a fullfilling life

Turn your affirmation into an intention by shifting the focus from a completed task to something you can practice.

My intention:

I am happy living a fullfilling life

Goals support intention. List a minimum of five goals.

My goals: *Embrace new technology*

1. *Create meaningful fu relationships by focusing on others, not myself.*
2. *be fit, healthy and maintain a 137 or so weight*
3. *Honor myself & my boundaries*

Now, let's get deeper. Answer the following questions.

How would your life be different if you lived by your intention?

How would your life change if your intention made your decisions for you?

Describe a relationship using intention as the foundation.

If you could create any intention what would it be?

Each time a question is presented to you, the opportunity to change your life is given. The questions above were created to wake you up to the possibilities that are available to you. For the next twenty-four hours I want you to live with your intention at the forefront of your mind. Write it down on a piece of colored paper and stick it on your bathroom mirror and on your desk at work. Evaluate how your day is going only by your intention. Use that as your measuring stick of success today. Nothing else. When you do that, you will be amazed at how much freedom you have to express more of your true self.

Day 6

Stretch, Risk, or Die

Jimmy and his mother, Carol, had not spoken to each other in two years. It all started when Jimmy moved to Las Vegas to work in the casinos. He always liked the bright lights, the wild crowds, and rubbing shoulders with the stars. But his mom didn't approve.

Carol thought that it wasn't the place to raise kids and besides, Carol's family owned a successful car dealership. She wanted Jimmy to be a part of it. As Jimmy packed his car to drive across country, the accusations started flying, terrible things were said, and feelings were hurt. Carol was devastated and felt betrayed. Jimmy thought his mother was selfish and judgmental.

I met Jimmy when he attended my Fearless Foundation Weekend. He shared how his relationship with his mother was now negatively affecting his upcoming marriage. He wanted his mother to be at the wedding and so did his future wife, but no one would make the first move. Realizing it was time to deal with his mother was one thing, doing something about it was another. Jimmy needed the tools to help him take the first steps toward reconciliation. I asked him if he was ready to "stretch, risk, or die."

Stretch, Risk, or Die is an exercise I created to help you gain perspective on the challenges that confront you. It helps identify the fears that keep you stuck, by labeling each potential action outside your comfort zone as a stretch, risk, or die. Think of it this way: The more fear associated with an action—with stretch representing the least amount of fear and a die the most—the more vulnerable you will feel and the more reactive your behavior might be. It is valuable to understand how you determine a stretch, risk, or die so you can learn to make the best decision possible.

Stretch, Risk, or Die looks like this:

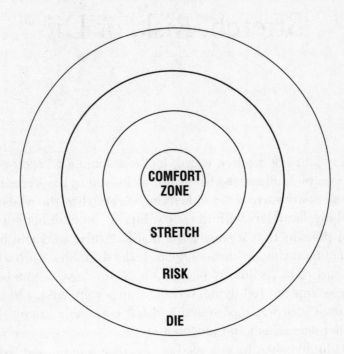

Notice your comfort zone is surrounded by three levels of fear. When you take an action that you have avoided but that isn't necessarily hard, you are at the first level of fear, called a "stretch." Breaking through to the next level of fear is a "risk." Most of the actions that you will take that will change your life will be categorized as a risk. And lastly, if you do something so scary that it makes you feel like a part of you is going to die, you have stepped into the "die" zone. The die zone usually consists of situations that you have successfully avoided for a certain period of time or that you would never even think of getting involved in.

A stretch is something you do that is associated with your lowest level of fear, but regardless, it does take you out of your comfort zone. It is a small step that pushes you into the unknown. For instance, let's say you have been single for six years and have started to think about dating again. The first time you allowed yourself to even think about dating, that might be considered a stretch. Another stretch could be smiling at someone you are attracted to. Notice I didn't say "talk" or "flirt." I said "smile." A "smile" is a stretch, where "talking" or "flirting" might be considered more scary. For most people smiling does not feel as vulnerable as talking or flirting, therefore it would be a "stretch."

A risk is something that takes courage to accomplish. Perhaps you have been thinking of doing more than smiling at some attractive strangers; you want to make the move and start to date. If asking your friends to set you up on a blind date is more nerve-racking than smiling, then it would be a risk. A risk carries the possibility of rejection and failure. You might get hurt, feel stupid, or get frustrated, but the end result is always worth the risk. The result is called self-confidence.

When you feel like you are going to die if you take the next step, you are in the die zone. If you believe only losers need help with dating, then signing up for an Internet dating service would bring all those fears to the surface. You'd make up convincing excuses why you shouldn't date.

It's normal to want to avoid anything that would make you feel like you are going to die. It is that feeling that stops you from moving forward. When I first thought of getting a divorce, I thought I was going to "die." I didn't want a divorce. It felt wrong. I was afraid of what it would mean, how it would change my life. I was devastated at the thought, let alone the ordeal of actually going through with it. But in reality, if I was going to be true to myself I would have to be willing to let go of the known, and step into the unknown. It feels like you are never going to be the same. And that is the good news.

Now, a stretch for one person could be a risk for another. All stretch, risk, or dies are different for different people. Never compare your fears to another's. It can't be done.

To give you some more examples, after my parents' deaths I felt like I was going to die if I forgave myself. I had a ton of reasons why I didn't deserve to be free of the guilt. A stretch was hanging photos of my parents up on my wall. A risk was telling people the truth of how my parents died. For years I lied about it, afraid no one would like me if they knew my father was a murderer. My fear of rejection gave me permission to wiggle out of telling the truth to just about anyone.

Jimmy had to face his mother. It was time to decide what actions he could take as he identified his fears by labeling them stretch, risk, or die. We brainstormed ways he could reconnect that included: write a letter, create a photo album for his parents with pictures of his life in Vegas, call home and ask to speak to Mom, a surprise visit home, ask Mom about what kind of car he should buy, invite his parents to come to Vegas for the weekend, get his mother tickets to one of the car shows in town and send a plane ticket, apologize, forgive his mother, send a wedding invitation, call his dad and ask him to invite Mom, just forget it, have a bridal shower and invite them to come, have a wedding reception in his hometown.

I asked Jimmy to label all his options either a stretch, risk, or a die.

Jimmy quickly put "Ask Mom about what kind of car he should buy" under stretch. He knew that would be the least threatening way to approach his mom. "Send a wedding invitation" seemed like a risk because it didn't feel quite right to send it without warning. Maybe his mother would feel slighted and get angrier. Jimmy was surprised that "Just forget it" felt like a "die." He hadn't realized how much of an emotional toll it had been to be disconnected from his mother.

I pointed out that unresolved issues become a burden on our well-being whether we are conscious of it or not. Jimmy had been trying to pretend it didn't affect him, but when I asked him if it was okay that his mother might not be at his wedding, he knew the answer was no. It wouldn't be okay. They had too many good memories to bury their relationship under this one major disagreement. As Jimmy and I talked it out, it became clear that without this reconciliation, Jimmy would not live "happily ever after."

Taking actions produces consequences, and labeling something a "die" means we think dire consequences are a given. We convince ourselves that something will go horribly wrong. But we are making all of that up. We don't know. We are just guessing. I asked Jimmy why he never stretched himself during this silent period. He told me that he knew if he extended his hand in reconciliation, it would force him to deal with all the issues he'd had in the past with his mother.

He didn't want to go there. He wasn't betting on her being her best, he counted on her acting her worst.

It was time to act. Jimmy chose a stretch: create a photo album of his life in Vegas. It would take time, but he hoped it would help his mother come to terms with his move and his upcoming wedding. He started to take pictures on a Saturday afternoon. Photos of his garden, his favorite restaurant—the Cheesecake Factory—and his future wife all made the album. In all he put thirty photos in a beautiful brown leather album and wrote a card that said *Thank you*. Jimmy admitted it was time to put the past behind, quit blaming his mother, and start to mend their relationship.

Last I heard, his mother had come out to Vegas to meet his fiancee and all went fairly well. Jimmy and his mother discussed their different lifestyles, and both of them spoke about their desire to heal their relationship. On the day of his wedding he had the two most important women in his life there: his wife and his mother.

Name an area of your life that would have to change in order for you to be more true to yourself. Is it your career? Relationship? Health?

Area of change: _____
List five stretches you could take:

1.
2.
3.
4.
5.

List five risks you could take:

1.
2.
3.
4.
5.

List five actions you could take that would feel so scary, you would feel like a part of you is dying:

1.

2.

3.

4.

5.

Now it's your turn. Go ahead and plot your stretch, risk, and dies below.

Having a visual picture helps put things into perspective. For Jimmy it made his hidden fears visible and nothing, once revealed, is as scary as you think. I asked Jimmy to take one stretch a day and, when he was ready, to take a risk and then go for a "die." I am asking you to do the same.

Remember to ask a friend for support while you are moving through your fears. It is normal to want to run when you feel vulnerable. But the true you never wants to hide. Face your life. Face your fears. Stretch. Risk. And be willing to kill off your old negative, confining thoughts. It will feel like a part of you is dying, and it is.

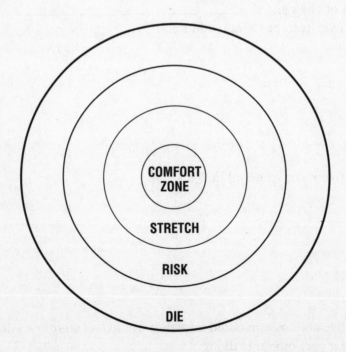

The part that no longer serves you. The part that keeps you stuck. That part that fear controls. Let it go.

Today, Stretch, Risk, or Die

Please answer the following questions to the best of your ability. The answers will lead you to the next action step necessary to change your life.

If you stretched each day, how would your life change?

What stretch, risk, or die must you take in order to change your life?

What stretch, risk, or die have you ignored that's stopping you from being true to yourself?

Which stretch, risk, or die do you want to avoid at all costs?

Are You Making It Up
or Is It True?

elly was a raven beauty who strutted into my office wearing a crème silk suit and a determined expression. She had hired me the day before to make her dreams come true. No ifs, ands, or buts. Dream making was serious business to Kelly. And she had a lot of dreams.

Her dream list included surrounding herself with more supportive friends. She had read my first book, *Fearless Living,* and knew how fanatical I was about the importance of support. Things such as: "No one can be fearless alone" or "No one person can satisfy all your needs—that's where good friends come in" or "Love is easier when you can share your joys and sorrows with a friend" were ringing in her ears when she arrived for our first appointment.

Hesitant to confess that she had few to no actual friends, Kelly tried to convince me her friends were the problem, not her. She told me some stories that were hard to believe, such as how her ex–best friend was secretly in love with her boyfriend and tried to steal him away or how a past friend purposely spilled a drink in her lap at the office Christmas party the previous year or the time she had asked a friend for help and he just flatly said no. As I sat listening to story after story, I silently wondered how every single friend could be so inconsiderate and selfish. Could it be true? Sure, it could. But I doubted it.

When I was younger and unsure of who I was, I, too, went through friends like water going through a sieve. I could barely keep them in my life for more than six months. Convinced that no one would ever understand me or really like me, I set up impossible tasks to test their love before I ever got close. I asked them to think of me before themselves, agree with my opinions, and have the same enemies I had. Because isn't that what friends should do? Boy, was I wrong.

Not that my friends didn't want to help me—they just had their own lives to worry about. But back then I needed them to be true to me rather than to themselves. Any lack of attention felt like a betrayal, and I wasn't going to put up with it. I would dump a friend at the mere hint that she would pick someone over me, didn't agree with me, or didn't call back pronto. Victimized by my lack of support, I would wail on and on about how I gave so much and my so-called friends would just take and take and take.

I was loaded with insecurities, but I didn't see it that way. I had convinced myself that my friends were the problem. They weren't loyal enough, giving enough, loving enough. Of course I rated myself an A+ in all of those categories. I didn't see any connection between cutting them out of my life and my lack of self-acceptance. I just thought I had to take care of myself, and I couldn't be bothered with all these people emotionally draining me.

My friends didn't have a chance. Neither did hers.

"Are you making it up or is it true?" I asked. I had stopped Kelly midsentence.

"What do you mean? Of course it's true," she said with great irritation. "I thought you were supposed to be on my side."

"Oh, I am, Kelly," I retorted. "Yet, being on your side doesn't mean I will always agree with you. So again, answer the question. Are you making it up or is it true?"

"Which story are you asking about?" It was a stall tactic.

"Any story is fine. Pick your ex–best friend if you would like. Was she really trying to steal your boyfriend away? Honestly?"

Asking the tough questions is my job, and I relish the opportunity to help my clients see the light regarding how their false perceptions give them permission to make decisions that are basically built on lies. Lies we tell ourselves so we don't have to confront a friend, or ask for help or face embarrassment. Many of us would rather kill off friends than face the truth. I was asking Kelly to face the truth. It was up to her if she was going to come clean and be fearless or get stuck hiding behind her mask. I was silent. I was going to wait it out.

After what seemed like hours, she finally spoke with a voice that was barely audible. "I don't know. I thought so."

Whenever I hear *I thought so,* it tells me that you don't know, you aren't sure, and you're guessing. Guessing doesn't build intimacy, it builds walls. Kelly was so scared to find out the real reason behind her relationship problems that she chose to conveniently blame her friends.

Now for all of you who are thinking, Well, what if there was a grain of truth in her stories? Well, let's say Kelly's ex–best friend did flirt with her boyfriend. Are you telling me that it was purposeful, manipulative, and evil, or was it harmless, fun, and playful? Kelly's level of security in her relationship would determine that answer. And more important, Kelly wasn't willing to have a truthful conversation with her friend to find out her intentions.

Kelly's look of confidence was just an act; inside she was scared to death that she wasn't lovable. She unconsciously started to look for excuses why her boyfriend would leave her. Accusing her boyfriend of lying to her became a mode of operation for Kelly. She just kept pushing and testing him until eventually he did leave.

One of the main reasons we turn a small situation into a huge problem is to justify our feelings. We feel bad, so there must be a reason. Aha! Best friend flirting with boyfriend. That's it. And off we go, taking innocent gestures and turning them into evil acts of betrayal.

Think of the people who have betrayed you. Are you sure they betrayed you? Did they plan on hurting you? Were you the target all along? Or was it an innocent action executed on one of your bad days?

Kelly had to be honest with herself. To gain perspective it was time to separate facts from fiction, i.e., what actually happened versus her interpretation. To help her gain confidence and deeper intimacy I asked her why she didn't ask her boyfriend and her friend about their intentions rather than getting angry and blaming first. Bottom line, Kelly needed to gather facts. I understand that when emotions are running high, facts and fiction appear to be the same, but they are not. One is the truth and one is fabricated from bits and pieces to create a new reality.

When we make things up about the way people feel or think, it only confirms our low self-worth. The woman in the corner of the room giving you a dirty look probably isn't even looking at you. She's probably just thinking a thought in your direction. You got passed by for a promotion. Does your boss really hate you or did it happen for another reason altogether? Are you willing to ask for an explanation or is it easier to just brush it away with the handy excuse "My boss doesn't like me"? What about your last failed relationship? Did they break your heart on purpose? Were they a jerk? Name calling is a good indication that you are taking things personally. When that happens, it is so easy to fabricate a reason why they are treating you that way. Of course, it's rarely something you did. I love it when I hear people use the rationalization "They are just jealous." Oh, please! Perhaps one percent of the time that would be true, but I believe accusing someone of jealousy is just an easy out. There doesn't have to be any real conversation, only condemnations. That doesn't help make dreams come true. I guarantee that it tears them apart.

I am embarrassed to admit that I have found myself acting that way over traffic. Take for instance that last time I drove on the 405 freeway in Los Angeles. A green pickup truck with chrome hubcaps cut in front of me at sixty-five miles an hour. My first reaction was "I can't believe that guy. What a jerk. Who does he think he is?"

When I have a reaction that is disproportionate to the event, I always stop and ask myself: Am I making it up or is it true? So I asked. The answer: I was totally making it up. I was already angry about something that happened that morning but I was trying to ignore it. The other driver just became my scapegoat. The minute I realized what was happening I asked myself: What else could be true?

That question is designed to help you put your emotions to the side while giving you time to contemplate new perspectives. When you come up with only one rationale for anyone's behavior it proves you want to be right more than you want to be open. Focus on expanding your creativity by coming up with at least three reasons. It isn't about excusing their behavior, it is about understanding it and allowing yourself to see things differently.

Perhaps he didn't notice my car because I was in his blind spot. What if he was trying to get someplace fast like the hospital? Maybe his mind was distracted because he was fired from his job. And so on. Allowing myself to brainstorm other reasons that his car pulled out in front of me is an exercise in compassion. It helps me to see the driver as innocent.

Notice I didn't make up a negative reason that would have attacked the driver like "Maybe he is just trying to push his weight around" or "He must be really insecure" or "He is just not a good driver." I didn't put him down to make myself feel better. If I am going to make something up, it might as well empower me. Putting someone else down does not make me feel good about myself. Being creative, compassionate, and understanding does.

Be willing to give up the security of making up things for a life filled with intimacy. You can't get close to anyone if you aren't willing to have a conversation that might lead to disagreements. Making things up keeps you isolated and right. Asking clarifying questions gives you the opportunity to connect instead of judge.

I realize that it is a simple example, yet simple is the perfect place to start. Things become more emotional and more important the closer something is to you. When that is true, it is hard to have perspective and the courage to ask: Am I making it up or is it true?

Today, Practice Being True

You want to change your life? Answer the following questions to find out what is true or false in your life.

Why can't you be true to yourself?

What excuses do you make up when things don't go your way?

What things are you making up about the people you love? (Just because you think your father doesn't love you doesn't mean it is true. Check your emotions at the door and focus on facts and facts alone.)

List the emotions that you feel when you make things up about people. For instance, perhaps someone looks at you and turns away.

You feel rejected. Do you make up a story about the person (they are jealous, selfish, etc.)?

If you had to ask yourself, Am I making this up or is this true, before you could speak, how would your life change?

Learning what situations trigger your urge to make things up will allow you to address the reason you do it. When you make things up, it is a defense mechanism. You have to decide to give up that defense and focus on the facts rather than relying on how you feel. Paying attention to the feelings that go with the impulse to fictionalize will help you wake up to which emotions cause you to go into protect mode. If you are serious about changing your life, you'll have to be honest with yourself about when you do and don't see the truth inside the experience.

For the next twenty-four hours, anytime you become irritated, ask yourself: Am I making it up or is it true? Ask the question and be honest about the answer. When you are willing to be truthful, you can change the way you think. Making things up only keeps you stuck in your fears and frustrations. It gives no answers but instead shuts the door to your future, whether that includes a new job, a new love, or a new you.

If you are ready to accelerate your growth, focus on the facts below:

- Are you making it up or is it true? Keeps you honest and open with others.
- When you make things up, you are afraid to become vulnerable and therefore intimate.
- See the situation "as is," taking your perceptions out and focusing on the facts.
- Facing when you make things up will help you to heal.

Day 8

The Freedom of Discipline

Today was Nicky's birthday and she wasn't happy about turning fifty. She came to me to get some help with her consulting business. *Floundering* was the word she used to describe it, but Nicky did not look like she was floundering. She was dressed to impress. Her tight-fitting gray-flecked sweater showed off her toned physique. To finish the look she wore gray flannel pleated pants with a chrome belt that looked like it had cost a fortune. She seemed to be doing very well, except she was sitting here telling me her business was going under . . . fast.

I needed some perspective. I asked her to define two words that I knew would give me the answers I needed. I invite you to define them for yourself.

Define *freedom:*

Define *discipline:*

When I was struggling in my business I defined these two words for myself and the answers shocked me. I defined *discipline* as "confining and rigid," while *freedom* was "doing whatever I want whenever I want to." I remembered that as I took a peek at Nicky's definitions.

Nicky's definition of *freedom:*
Being able to take a vacation when I want to. Owning three houses. Getting my pilot's license. Working wherever suits me. No ties, strings, or restrictions. Taking care of my needs.

Nicky's definition of *discipline:*
No spontaneity. Doing what is required. Going back to school. People telling me what to do. Being bored. Waking up at the same time every day. Eating six small meals a day.

I wasn't surprised. Nicky had the classic symptoms of someone wanting the trappings of success but being unwilling to work for them. Many people are held back by their lack of understanding of what true discipline takes and what real freedom gives.

True discipline takes heightened awareness and self-mastery. In the past I thought if I followed a daily schedule I was sacrificing freedom. I didn't understand that, in reality, there is no such thing as sacrifice. There are only choices. Learning the value of discipline taught me how to make consistent choices that continually empower me. My decisions are no longer all over the place, they are focused, clear, and consistent.

Nicky needed a dose of discipline. I asked her if she was willing to take responsibility for her business failing. She tried to sell me on the fact that her customers were demanding and fussy, so no one could win them over. It wasn't her, she assured me, it was them.

That wasn't going to work with me. I asked her again. Are you willing to take full responsibility for your business going under? If she was, there was hope. If she didn't, she was going to continue the cycle of success and failure.

While Nicky was pondering her answer, I put away my pen and paper and shoved my arm through the sleeve of my leather coat.

"Okay," she said. "It's my fault. I guess I don't want to work that much. I always thought working for yourself was the easy way to riches, but I guess I was wrong."

I sat down and looked her in the eye and said, "It is time to get to work."

I explained to Nicky that discipline was the key to freedom. In actuality, freedom could not be attained without it. True freedom includes an ability to focus, an inner peace, self-acceptance, and clarity of intention. Things that cannot be obtained without the rigors of applied discipline.

Years ago I rebelled against discipline just as Nicky had. I wanted freedom, and being a child of the sixties, my definition of freedom was needing nothing but love. But I soon found out love wasn't going to be enough, especially since I had a hard time believing anyone loved me (because I didn't love myself) or trusted me (because I could not count on myself) or thought I was good enough (because I didn't either). I wanted proof of love without intimacy. I wanted results without consistent hard work. I wanted to be given responsibility before I earned it. I wanted it because I thought I deserved it. I was one of those typical people who cried when she didn't get a break but never did anything to make the opportunity happen.

When I was a waitress in my twenties, I used to complain incessantly about my boss because I was convinced I knew more than he did. Whether I was right or not wasn't the point. I wanted all the benefits of management yet didn't want the long hours or the low pay. I made more in tips in a week than my boss did in his paycheck. I didn't care if it wasn't fair. I figured that since I had the highest sales of any waitress in the place, I should get extra benefits like being able to come in late or cut out of work early. I wanted to be treated like the owner of the restaurant without doing the work of getting there. I thought I deserved it.

I always find the word *deserving* fascinating. Usually the folks who actually "deserve" it don't ask for it from anyone else, they are busy going out and getting it for themselves.

The folks who think they do "deserve" it are usually so focused on what they aren't receiving from others, whether it is respect or money, they aren't getting down to business. That was me in the restaurant. I was so busy complaining about the management's lack of appreciation, I couldn't get on with my life and find the work I was meant to do. My pettiness kept me from finding my purpose.

Deserving success without discipline would not have been the kind of freedom I truly craved. It would have been empty. In fact, my life was empty until I realized the only way to obtain freedom is through self-discipline. I began to understand that self-discipline would give me the tools and skills I required to succeed, and I would be doing what needed to be done. In the long run, that would give me the confidence to count on myself. I grew up, and that was an important step in my healing. My mantra became: True freedom lies within the lessons of self-discipline.

Now I had to put Nicky on a discipline regime. She wouldn't like it at first, but I knew that within three months she would see the benefit and feel a freedom that, until now, had only been a fantasy.

I asked Nicky how many hours a day she worked, what did she work on, what distracted her, what kept her focused, what turned her on and off, what were her monetary goals, how many clients she had, etc.

When all my questions were answered, Nicky told me she had never before so thoroughly examined her business. Answering the hard questions can take its toll emotionally. Who wants to face their fear of failure? But Nicky hung in there like a trouper. It was then I knew she was willing to be true to herself.

I asked Nicky to complete a Life Log, a daily list of her hour-by-hour activities. I also wanted her to keep track of which activities ignited her passion and if the activity moved her business forward.

I gave her symbols to make it easy. At the top of each box I asked her to write the specific activity. Below that her job was to determine if the activity would be labeled a P for passion or NP for no passion, as well as deciding if it deserved an arrow up to symbolize moving her business forward or an arrow down to denote decrease in business. Also, I asked her to add up her working hours versus play hours.

To assure her that it wasn't about all business and no play, I emphasized that taking care of herself in moderation would eventually support an increase in business. We agreed to meet in one week.

I invite you to fill out the Life Log on the next page to find out how you are spending your time. If your career is fine and love is the reason you are reading this book, you can do the exercise with one modification. Instead of an arrow indicating an increase in business, the arrow can point to an increase of love in your life.

TIMES	Monday	Tuesday	Wednesday
6:00 A.M. P/NP ↑↓			
7:00 A.M. P/NP ↑↓			
8:00 A.M. P/NP ↑↓			
9:00 A.M. P/NP ↑↓			
10:00 A.M. P/NP ↑↓			
11:00 A.M. P/NP ↑↓			
Noon P/NP ↑↓			
1:00 P.M. P/NP ↑↓			
2:00 P.M. P/NP ↑↓			
3:00 P.M. P/NP ↑↓			
4:00 P.M. P/NP ↑↓			
5:00 P.M. P/NP ↑↓			

Thursday	Friday	Saturday	Sunday

TIMES	Monday	Tuesday	Wednesday
6:00 P.M. P/NP ↑↓			
7:00 P.M. P/NP ↑↓			
8:00 P.M. P/NP ↑↓			
9:00 P.M. P/NP ↑↓			
10:00 P.M. P/NP ↑↓			
11:00 P.M. P/NP ↑↓			
Midnight P/NP ↑↓			
1:00 A.M. P/NP ↑↓			
2:00 A.M. P/NP ↑↓			
3:00 A.M. P/NP ↑↓			
4:00 A.M. P/NP ↑↓			
5:00 A.M. P/NP ↑↓			

Thursday	Friday	Saturday	Sunday

After one week Nicky was surprised by the direction of her arrows. Most were pointing down. She admitted that whenever she was jabbering on the phone to a friend or an acquaintance she used to rationalize it by telling herself, You never know. I pointed out that there is truth in that because you never know where your business can come from, but talking to your friends about the party on Saturday most likely will not increase the number of consulting contracts. Her total working time added up to forty-one hours while her play time equaled thirty-five. The rest was divvied up between sleep and necessary maintenance tasks such as showering.

"At least I am balanced," Nicky quipped. I was unimpressed.

I appreciated her commitment to a balanced lifestyle, but I suspected it wasn't something she did consciously. She was just drawn to play first and almost had to force herself to work. That was clear on her ratio of passionate versus nonpassionate activities. NP far outweighed P.

Nicky had a choice. She could either turn her play into a money-making venture or focus on creating more passion in her present career. I asked her to choose. She had an interesting answer.

"If I make money at play, it won't feel like play. It will take the fun out of it. I want to keep my play and work separate." Nicky seemed clear on this point.

It was an interesting perspective. I wasn't convinced she was telling the truth, but as always I focus on what the client wants to make happen. My theory is, Let's "act as if" Nicky is telling the truth because if we do, the results and her attitude will prove whether it is true or false soon enough.

With her focus on discipline, business was a priority. I asked her to find a friend to help her brainstorm things she could do. Together, they came up with a list of activities that could increase her business opportunities, such as network meetings, joining the chamber of commerce, redesigning her Web site, etc.

With her list in hand she started to commit to one activity a week. First she joined the chamber and volunteered to help with their membership drive. Next, she held an open house at her office and invited all her past clients. As she became accountable to others, she felt a surge of confidence. And then it hit her: She was mixing business and pleasure effortlessly.

At our next meeting she could barely contain her excitement. Nicky had always thought chamber meetings and networking organizations were for losers. She had no idea the benefit these types of activities could give her, such as connecting her to other business owners, meeting new potential business clients, and feeling like part of a group.

"I never realized before how I used play to avoid business. I never knew focusing on discipline could be so much fun," said Nicky.

As she started to mix business and pleasure, she naturally found herself being more accountable because it was something she loved. Holding herself accountable and showing up for the weekly networking meetings and volunteering regularly at the chamber had opened a door for Nicky. Through becoming more disciplined she used her time wisely and started to think of the big picture rather than just making decisions based on her mood. What was really neat is she found her passion again and her business started to take off, all because she was willing to put more on her plate, not less. Discipline helped her accomplish everything more easily than she had ever imagined.

Are you disciplined?

Today, Practice Disciplined Freedom

Learning more about how you live your life right now is an opportunity to find out where you are true to yourself. The more information you have, the more you will be inspired to change your life.

Can you count on yourself to finish a task that you started?

How many projects are left undone in your home right now?

What would your life look like if you were disciplined?

What could you accomplish if you were disciplined?

Being truthful with yourself is an important step in self-discovery. I don't think people lie to themselves on purpose, but in truth we do make up reasons why we can't or can do things. Discipline gets a bad rap and our dreams go by the wayside.

Understanding the difference between discipline and freedom will give you the assurance you need to do what must be done with less fear. Your willingness to become more disciplined tells me how committed you are to being true to yourself and changing your life. Focus on one area of your life at a time or on building one skill at a time. This will support you in becoming disciplined without getting overwhelmed. Be sure to acknowledge your progress.

Day 9

Shine Your Light

At forty-three years old Jessica was the assistant manager of a restaurant chain in Houston. Her boss, Todd, had been promoted to the regional office and everyone thought that Jessica was a shoo-in for the job. But two days before Todd left, Jessica found out that they were bringing in a thirty-year-old hotshot from Atlanta to take Todd's place.

Being passed up for the promotion was hard. She tried to pretend she was okay but in reality she wasn't. She became short-tempered and difficult to work with, complaining endlessly about all her hard work she had done for nothing. This rejection felt like a slap in the face.

Working with Jessica was beginning to feel a lot like walking on eggshells. It was becoming very painful for her employees. That's where I came in. It was time for Jessica to learn how this had happened and what, if anything, she had or had not done to contribute.

Shining your light takes courage. It isn't easy to say "I did it" loud enough for the world to hear. Fear usually stops you from sharing your accomplishments, revelations, or transformations. Instead, it tells you to minimize, ignore, or devalue your endeavors. It tells you it isn't humble. Being egotistical is one of the worst names you can be called, along with bigheaded. Imagine someone calling you selfish and you will have an inkling of how hard it might be for you to shine your light.

When we are fighting to be our better, truer self we must not forget to honor our accomplishments and the risks we have taken. We must not forget to move forward despite our fears. We must not forget that feeling bad about ourselves does not make excuses valid; it just makes the lives we live smaller.

Rarely do we let our light shine. Usually our fear of being rejected covers up our good intentions and we stay stuck to our negative thoughts, feelings, and opinions. We are more likely to applaud someone else shining than ourselves. It can be difficult getting past your superstitions and concerns, but it is necessary if you want to reach your full potential and be true to yourself.

Imagine you are Jessica. What would you be saying to yourself right now? For the most part you would have some choice words to say such as, "I can't believe you blew it" or "You are never going to get anywhere in this company." Beating yourself up would be the order of the day and the sad part is you would think you deserve the punishment. You didn't give enough. You weren't on top of things. You didn't do your best. When nothing you do seems to matter, your light dims. It starts to feel dark in your heart and you can feel alone, abandoned, or betrayed.

Maybe you don't judge yourself during these difficult moments but instead blame the boss or compare yourself with the hotshot. Both of these choices only prove how scared you are, but you do them anyway to justify the pain.

What if you've given up judging, comparing, and blaming? Now what would you do if you were Jessica? The answer still might not include shining your light. It is usually the last thing on people's minds. But what if shining your light could put things in perspective and build your confidence?

I am not talking about bragging or sharing a list of your accomplishments with strangers. Countless times someone has sent me an e-mail or greeting card with their resume attached touting how they can save me. That doesn't work for me. I want to be treated as an equal who needs support, not someone who is defective.

Shining your light does not mean you think you can save anybody. If you think you can, quit reading. You don't need this book.

I had a feeling Jessica didn't get the promotion because her boss wasn't impressed. Not that Jessica didn't do some impressive things. Her boss just never heard about it.

We hesitate to shine our light because we fear that if we shine we will stop someone else from shining. That isn't true. Your light does not take away from another. There is enough light to go around. In reality, when we dim our own light we can dissuade others from shining. When you think nothing matters or you waste your time comparing, rationalizing, or minimizing, you are dimming your light. It doesn't help anyone. Everyone needs support to shine, and if you're willing to shine, it gives others the courage to do so as well.

Shining your light could be as simple as being happy no matter what mood anyone else is in. It could be acknowledging your accomplishments as they happen rather than years down the road. Being proud of yourself is an important aspect of shining your light. Sharing your feelings with another and allowing someone to get to know you is telling the world you are willing to shine.

Wearing clothes that make you feel fabulous is another aspect of shining your light. Being willing to look and feel your best is part of putting your best foot forward, a necessary step in shining your light. Little things like getting your nails done might give you more courage to shine. Taking care of your physical presence while you are cultivating your skills on the inside will help you stay focused on being true to yourself.

I suggested to Jessica that a great way to shine her light at work would be to e-mail a weekly update to her boss about all the changes she'd be making for the betterment of the company. It could include how she had handled a particular problem, her opinions about the work environment, and her praise about employees. As always, I asked her to be specific. If she wrote in generalities, her message would be less effective.

If you are committed to helping others shine their light, give specific compliments frequently. At work, send letters of acknowledgment to a coworker and her boss. Let the office know that you appreciate the hard work someone is doing. You could even start an Employee of the Month reward program. Apply this to your home and watch your mate and children shine.

I pointed out to Jessica that if you want credit, you must be willing to ask for it. She wanted that promotion but she secretly believed she would just get it without sharing her wins. Your ability to share your wins determines your willingness to shine.

I asked Jessica to list her top three wins. You do the same.

1.
2.
3.

"The last issue of our company's newsletter named our store the most improved. Our sales have been steadily increasing since we opened two years ago. That was a huge win for me. Another win was the staff I hired. Overall I think I did a good job. My last win is personal. I signed up for an Internet dating service last week. I am so embarrassed that I haven't been dating anyone, but my friend Tanya talked me into it. We did it together. That is a huge win for me. Well, I hope it is."

Keeping track of your wins is crucial to building your self-esteem. It doesn't matter if they are personal or professional, a win is a win. Being willing to give yourself credit for the things you accomplish will give you more permission to shine because your value will increase and your worth will be validated.

Next, I asked Jessica to name three compliments she would love to receive about herself. Please write down what compliments would make a difference in your life.

1.
2.
3.

Jessica explained her answers. "Just yesterday I created a whole new system to deal with complaints. Has anyone noticed? No. Last year I fought to get Susan, our top-selling waitress, a raise and she got it. I think I have good negotiation skills that have gone unnoticed. Oh, and a customer last week told me the restaurant was beautiful. To be honest, when she said that to me, it felt like a stab in my heart. No one has told me I am beautiful for a long, long time."

It is amazing how often we yearn to get our needs met but refuse to ask for what we need. Secretly we believe that someone should just magically know what we need and fulfill it. But life doesn't work that way. If you want to be noticed, you must be willing to shine, and asking for the compliments that would support your self-confidence is something that you must be willing to do.

I do that when I am feeling low. I call my friend Marta and ask her to remind me how well I am doing and that my coaching is effective and my books help others. It was hard to do at first. It felt conceited and selfish. But I have come to realize my willingness to take care of my own needs helps me get back on track and keep shining.

Lastly, Jessica had to list three people she has refused to compliment even though they have earned it. Be truthful when you list the three folks you have refused to value.

1.
2.
3.

"This is hard. My top chef is amazing in the kitchen but has a bad attitude, so I never compliment him. I didn't think he deserved it. And Samantha, one of the hostesses, stayed three hours past her shift last week. I didn't bother to say anything, because she should want to stay. Tom was another person I thought of. He is my next-door neighbor who borrowed my mower when his broke down. He mowed my lawn along with his, but I haven't thanked him yet because he hasn't brought back my mower."

Jessica withheld compliments and gratitude from others because she wanted their intentions to be pure and to be treated just right. She never gave a compliment unless the job was done to her specifications and with the right attitude.

"I don't want to be taken advantage of," she claimed. "I don't want to be one of those women that get walked on."

I understood her position, but her unwillingness to appreciate others kept others away and also kept her from giving herself the credit she had earned. If everything wasn't perfect, it didn't count. How can you shine with so many rules standing in the way? You have to do it perfectly, have a great attitude, and follow Jessica's unspoken rules. No one was winning, including Jessica. Her promotion was dependent on approval from her boss, but she hadn't patted her staff on the back, or herself. No one was able to shine.

Refusing to give someone a compliment that they have earned, you are in essence denying yourself the permission to shine. When you help others shine their light, and when you shine your light, others will have more courage to follow suit. Whether you believe me or not, shining your light and sharing little wins does give other people permission to shine. Imagine your coworker sharing his latest time-saving tip or a friend telling you about her latest discovery. That's shining. Shining gives you: permission to enjoy life. Permission to be passionate. Permission to be excited about what you do and who you are.

It is hard to keep your enthusiasm going when you aren't able to share it. That's what happened to Jessica. She had quit showing how much she cared because she didn't feel appreciated. She stopped sharing her opinions, ideas, and wins with her boss. She thought it didn't matter anymore. But it did. If not to her boss, it did for the sake of her own soul.

Imagine you are meeting God at the pearly gates of heaven. He is asking you one question and one question only to determine if you are getting into heaven or living in hell. The question is: During your life were you willing to shine your light for all to see? When you shine, you give the world hope. When you shine, you are saying you matter. When you shine, the world is set free.

In the beginning, be willing to shine whether you believe it or not. With practice you will begin to believe that you have value and worth and that being willing to shine will get you there. Shine!

Today Is Your Day to Shine!

I asked Jessica to answer the following questions. You do the same.

Blow your own horn. Name the last three pieces of good news you shared with your mate, friends, boss in the past month.

How do you feel when you share your good news?

What stops you from sharing good news?

What do you think will happen if you shine?

How do you feel when someone shares good news with you? Does it matter whether they are someone in your personal or professional life?

Understanding why you shine and what stops you from shining will tell you how you judge your value. But all we do is worthy of shining. Being willing to forgive yourself for having been being unable to shine in the past will clear away the guilt and shame that is clouding your vision. You can't shine if you don't see the good you do.

Remember, shining your light is a choice. It is the choice to make if you want to own your power and be empowering. Be willing to share your good news as well as give and receive compliments. When that happens, you will naturally shine. No effort will be required.

Day 10

Integration

Congratulations on making it to day ten. You are a third of the way through the journey.

On my journey to finding my true self I hit many roadblocks and barriers, just as I am sure that you have. There are so many personal things that you need to focus on. So many doubts and questions arise that you have never wanted to confront or answer. I have cried myself to sleep many nights in the face of the questions that you had to answer in these first ten days. I have questioned whether I am doing the right thing by trying to change my life. Is the pain and anguish I am dredging up from the bottom of my soul worth it? Maybe my life was better before I tried to change it?

The reason why I end each chapter with questions is because questions force answers. You are learning to answer the hard questions. Being true to yourself takes commitment, and commitment is hard.

But you have arrived at day ten and be proud of that.

Leslie had been working with me for about ten days when she became overwhelmed with the process of trying to change her life. I assured her that was normal. Focusing on yourself so intently can distort your perspective. Watching every word you say and every move you make can be alarming. Sometimes it can feel like you are worse off than when you started.

"Maybe I have done enough for right now," Leslie told me on day ten. "I am overloaded. I think I am making changes, but I don't know. Maybe this is enough change."

You have worked on everything from your confidence to understanding your purpose to learning how to find freedom in discipline. Those things alone could change a life. Just like Leslie you have been delving into the very core of your soul as we have been working together day in and day out. It is normal right about now to feel overwhelmed.

Let's stop for a moment and take a breath. Part of the reason we feel overwhelmed is that we have not integrated everything we have learned. It is in our head but not necessarily in our hearts and definitely not in our daily actions. When that happens, we can get frustrated. We know what we must do but we still don't do it consistently. It can remind us of our failures in the past and we can even say to ourselves, as Leslie did, "Maybe this is enough."

You will never stop changing. It is impossible. What can be frustrating is our seeming inability to integrate what we have learned. One sure way to integrate your insights is through your daily acknowledgments. When you acknowledge yourself you are admitting your changes and taking credit for them. Stopping for five minutes a day to pat yourself on the back is necessary to build your confidence and integrate insights and turn them into reality. When you acknowledge yourself you are saying, "Yes, I did it."

Recognizing all the insights you have had is the first step in integrating what you have learned. Insights are "aha" moments. And to ground those you must act on the insights immediately and acknowledge your willingness to do so. To make changes in your life permanent you must integrate what you have learned so it becomes a part of who you are.

Leslie's acknowledgments were as follows:

1. I acknowledge myself for asking myself daily: Am I making this up or is this true?
2. I acknowledge myself for buying fresh flowers as part of my commitment to passion.
3. I acknowledge myself for creating an intention that empowers me.
4. I acknowledge myself for writing acknowledgments every day.
5. I acknowledge myself for letting go of the falsehoods that have taken over my life.

Take a few minutes right now and acknowledge yourself five times for the changes you have made in the last ten days. Focus on the changes that have improved your life the most.

1.
2.
3.
4.
5.

Congratulations! With every change you make you are being more true to yourself.

Let's keep integrating. Tell me the three most life-changing revelations or insights you've had in the past ten days. For instance Leslie, after she discovered she was making up a lot in her relationships, went to her boyfriend, Gil, and apologized for all of the ways she'd stopped their love from growing because of her fear of being abandoned. Realizing she had been making things up was revolutionary. Her second most life-changing insight was how purpose was under her control. She had always thought her purpose was eluding her, but now that she sees purpose everywhere, she has quit feeling lost in her life. The third insight she had that made a huge impact on her was acknowledging that she had something special to share with the world.

Please list your three most revolutionary insights—the ones that made you say "aha." If you have more than three, please grab your personal journal or notebook and list as many as possible. Naming your insights makes them more real. It helps to shift them from just an insight to a way of being.

1.
2.
3.

Keep track of your insights on a regular basis. Write them down in the margins of the book or after each chapter or underline the sentence that precipitated the insight. Integrating what you have learned and turning it into what you know will give you courage to take bigger risks.

Taking risks is a confidence builder, and learning the difference between a stretch, risk, or die helps you gain perspective. Thinking about life through the stretch, risk, or die model will help you stay focused on where you want to go rather than how to stay safe. True safety lies in your ability to be comfortable being uncomfortable. Taking a stretch, risk, or die a day will help that become a way of life for you.

I want you to take a moment and give yourself credit. How many stretches have you taken in the past ten days? Risks? Have you been willing to do something so scary you feel like you are going to die? Identifying the ways in which you stretch, risk, and die is another way to acknowledge how hard you have been working to be true to yourself.

Leslie acknowledged that she stretched by calling her mother in the morning whether she wanted to or not, exercising one more time a week, and giving away some clothes that she had hoped she would fit into again. Her risks included telling her boyfriend, Gil, that she loved him every day, wearing a super sexy dress to an office party, and asking her boss for a meeting to discuss her salary the following week. Her die was actually having the meeting. She wanted to cancel it a hundred times. But she went regardless of how she was feeling and she stayed focused on finding the truth instead of fiction. The meeting was a success. She didn't get the raise she wanted, but she did get a title change and a year-end bonus.

Please list three stretches, three risks, and one die you were willing to take in the past ten days. I am not asking if things turned out okay or if you got what you wanted. That is not the purpose of stretching. Having the courage to be true to yourself is supported by the knowledge that you can stretch, risk, and die when you must rather than when your feelings give you permission or when things are guaranteed to go your way. This helps you learn to count on yourself regardless of how your day is going or what results you might get. That is true freedom.

Stretches:

1.
2.
3.

Risks:

1.
2.
3.

Die:

1.

Your willingness to do the work is evident based on your willing-ness to stretch, risk, and die. Change never happens in your comfort zone. Stop for a moment and acknowledge your courage. You are doing great.

You have been working on different aspects of yourself for the past ten days. The way you see the world has been challenged. The way you think and what you believe has been tested. I want you to be true to yourself as much as your courage will allow because being true to yourself takes a willingness to be fearless. Therefore, my commit-ment to you will give you more freedom, more confidence, more courage, so you can go anywhere you'd like, do anything you want, and meet anyone that you dare to.

Now, let's look at results. How has your life changed in the past ten days? Have people started treating you differently? Have you been able to speak up for yourself with more authority? Has living with in-tention helped keep you focused on what's important? When you ask yourself, "Are you making it up or is it true?" are you willing to hear any answer? What is your response or the response of the people around you?

Leslie's results included:

1. Gil's smile when she said "I love you" first.
2. Mom's friendly attitude when she called in the morning.

3. A stress-free sales luncheon with many compliments from the team.
4. Coworkers' comments about the fresh flowers on her desk. They were dying to know what was going on with her.
5. And of course, her title change and year-end bonus.

List five results you have noticed.

1.
2.
3.
4.
5.

Leslie couldn't believe the difference ten days could make in her life. Her desire to be true to herself was the catalyst, yet she had had no idea that so many things were making her so miserable.

"I always thought I was doing pretty good. I never understood why I wasn't always happy. I had a boyfriend, a good job, and a decent family, but things never seemed to fit. Life would work and then it wouldn't. The last ten days have shown me where I was putting myself down and how my fears were keeping me stuck. I can't wait for the next ten days. Let's keep going," Leslie said.

It was time to ground Leslie's shifts and changes one more time. To further anchor her to the changes she was making, I asked her to write a letter of gratitude to herself, from herself.

"A letter of gratitude? What do you mean to myself, from myself?" Leslie asked.

"I want you to write a letter beginning with 'Dear Leslie' and ending it with 'Love, Leslie.' This is a letter to you, from you. It is a thank-you letter for all of your hard work," I replied.

Writing a letter to yourself can seem awkward at first, but it is an important skill. I write letters to myself quite often. I imagine that it is the best part of myself, the true me, writing down her thoughts. It helps me stay focused on who I am without fear, without doubt.

Leslie took a few tries to get going. Remember, this is a letter of thanks. Leslie's letter began like this:

Dear Leslie,

Thanks for working so hard the past ten days on changing my life. I know it is helping me become a better person. I feel more powerful. I believe I am able to accomplish more. My self-esteem has improved. Thanks for asking me every day, "Am I making this up or is this true?" That sentence blows me away every time. . . .

Please start your letter with your first name and end it with your first name. Personalizing it will make it more real and will help you integrate what you have written. Take a few minutes and tell yourself how grateful you are for everything you are doing.

Dear _____,

Acknowledging yourself in letter form is another way to integrate the information you are gaining and make it more meaningful, more tangible. Turning concepts into reality is a process, and all things we have done today will help you do that with more ease.

I have one more exercise to help you give yourself credit for all of your changes. I would like you to rate yourself on a scale of one through ten on your ability to actualize the topics we have been working on together. One is the lowest score, ten is the highest.

For instance, we have discussed acknowledgments at great length as well as passion and purpose. How would you rate your ability to acknowledge yourself on a daily basis? Would you give yourself a two or a four or a seven? A two would mean you haven't given the concept much thought, a four would mean you are making an effort, while a seven tells me you are working hard at getting it.

Let's begin. I am going to list a series of skills and I want you to rate yourself on how much you have improved. This is another way to give yourself credit as well as a way to measure how you are doing so far. It will give you more guidance on which areas you need to focus on in the days ahead. This is not an opportunity to beat yourself up. That is not what this is about. It is about saying, "Yes, I know it, I am working on it, or I am living it." That's it.

Rate yourself on a scale of one through ten on your ability to actualize the following skills. We have talked about each one of these in the previous chapters. None are new to you. This is an opportunity to see how much you have grown in the last ten days. Imagine when you started these were all at zero. If you went up one point, you are moving forward.

"I rate my ability to embody _____ (topic) a _____ (score)."
Circle your score:

Skill	Rating											
Passion	Lowest	1	2	3	4	5	6	7	8	9	10	Highest
Purpose	Lowest	1	2	3	4	5	6	7	8	9	10	Highest
Intention	Lowest	1	2	3	4	5	6	7	8	9	10	Highest
Discipline	Lowest	1	2	3	4	5	6	7	8	9	10	Highest
Stretching	Lowest	1	2	3	4	5	6	7	8	9	10	Highest
Risking	Lowest	1	2	3	4	5	6	7	8	9	10	Highest
Die Zone	Lowest	1	2	3	4	5	6	7	8	9	10	Highest
Seeing Truth	Lowest	1	2	3	4	5	6	7	8	9	10	Highest
Confidence	Lowest	1	2	3	4	5	6	7	8	9	10	Highest
Shining	Lowest	1	2	3	4	5	6	7	8	9	10	Highest

To reiterate, if you have improved by one point you are doing fantastic. Change isn't measured by the rate of change, but by the permanence of continual growth. This is another way to acknowledge yourself in order to integrate all of your hard work.

You have been working hard, and today we are reflecting on your transformation. It is always good to take a step back and consider what you have done. It builds your confidence to take more risks in the future. It reminds you that change is possible. It allows you to see that you are willing to grow. All of that is necessary in order for you to move forward.

Being true to yourself is not always easy, but with the stronger foundation you have built for yourself today, it will become something that is attainable. For the rest of the day I would like you to revel in your changes. Your focus is integration. Pay attention to the skills you have gained in the last ten days. Find ways to use them, express them, share them.

At the end of your day, please review your letter of gratitude. Do you want to add anything to it? I am going to give you some space below just in case you want to write more things you are grateful for.

Dear _____,

Learning to be grateful in the moment will open your eyes to a world that is more loving, giving, and hopeful than you previously imagined. It will give you courage to keep facing your fears.

Day 11

Regrets

Valerie was a long-haired redhead who looked like she knew where she was going and how she was going to get there. She had recently realized that her career in banking no longer suited her eclectic personality, and went on to tell me that being true to herself was her top priority.

Becoming an interior decorator was her dream, but she didn't know if she should just go for it and open her own business or go back to school.

"But I can't afford to waste any more time," said Valerie. "I'm forty-three and I have to make the right decision."

I asked her what was her hurry, but she just kept repeating she didn't want to waste any more time. Time is so seductive. We want to act like it doesn't matter but we determine our success by it. How fast can we make the deal? How much can we make in a year? What did we accomplish in the last twelve months? Each January we are reminded to "get the most out of our year."

We can be ruled by time through our daily schedules and goal setting. If we try to ignore it, we are considered flaky or dropouts. If we say time isn't important, we are told we are a business risk. Who wants to work with someone who doesn't watch the clock? If we rely on the belief that "everything happens in perfect time," others fear we are complacent. It is easy to have a love/hate relationship with time.

Society is based on time. We use it every day to focus our attention on the tasks of the day. It tells us when to show up for work, when to eat lunch, and when to go home. We rely on time to tell us when we should get married and have children. We celebrate birthdays and anniversaries according to time. It is integral to our lives.

In reality there is plenty of time, but it doesn't seem so when you want something right away. One of my fundamental philosophies is that there is enough time for all I want to do. It just might not happen on my time schedule. I evaluate my success by my commitments rather than time. It takes the pressure off yet keeps the focus on what matters.

That wasn't true for Valerie. *Right decision* were two words she took seriously. She was convinced there was only one right choice. I wasn't. Many of my clients are addicted to being right and for many, time is their main driving force. I was sure Valerie had made many decisions in the past that she wasn't proud of.

Valerie wasn't a bad person for wanting to make the right choice—she was just a person who thought something bad would happen if she wasted any more time. When she finally had the courage to make a break from a career that confined her, she didn't want to experience any setbacks or frustration. She didn't want to make the wrong choice and get disappointed in herself all over again.

"Look, Rhonda, I don't have time to waste. I am getting older, so I must decide. Can you help me?"

I assured Valerie I would but first I wanted to know what was so bad about wasting time. She looked at me like I was crazy. "What is so bad about wasting time?" I repeated. "And what would happen to you if you did waste time?"

Valerie's desire to use her time productively was honorable, but it also caused sleepless nights and produced a rash on her back. She told me she could hear the clock ticking inside of her, taunting her with being a failure. Valerie had to use time wisely.

Valerie didn't trust. She didn't have faith. She didn't think time was on her side. She was convinced that time was against her. That came through clearly when she told me her age in the first three minutes of our first meeting. Obsession with completing a goal because of your age tells me you have regrets. Regrets in your past that you do not want to repeat.

We make mental notes about what we should be doing at certain times of our lives. And as we get older, it feels like time is speeding up. No more lollygagging. You get going and get successful before you hit thirty or you are a has-been. By twenty-five we should own our first house. By thirty we should find our purpose. By forty-five we should be able to retire. We feel we are being responsible when we line up our life along a timeline. We attach our wants to an age and tell ourselves it proves we are responsible. It is a good quality to have but not if time is the only thing that runs your life.

If we don't get things done on time, we are called procrastinators. If we are late for an appointment, we are told we are disrespectful. If we wait for the perfect time, we are told we are making excuses. We use our relationship with time to put ourselves down. But then again, we are assured that when we find our passion and do what we love, we will forget time exists. When love hits us, time won't matter. So here we are trying to master time but then are told, time is elusive when we are being true to ourselves.

Focusing on time and only time is faithless.

If you need to know what you are doing tomorrow today, there is little room for miracles. If you have to know if your business will be successful before it starts, there is little room for growth. If you have to be liked right away, there is no room for intimacy. How can you be true to yourself if time determines your every action?

Time is our friend if we use it properly. But we are its master, it does not master us. When I asked Valerie what was so wrong about wasting time, she told me that she had made bad decisions in the past, and because of that she was now years behind all of her friends. I asked her to be specific.

"When I was in my early twenties, I did things I'm not proud of."

"What things?" I asked.

"I'm embarrassed to say, but I drank too much and basically made bad decisions that cost me a lot of time."

"What bad decisions did you make?" I had to find out what was behind her drive to make the right choice.

"I dated men who weren't good for me. I quit school to follow my rock musician boyfriend around the country. Because of that I didn't finish college, and that's why I'm where I am today. I was so stupid." Her regret was palpable.

"Why was it stupid?" I asked. "Weren't you just trying to be loved?"

"Well, yes. I suppose so. But it didn't get me anywhere, did it?"

Valerie wouldn't let her past go. Valerie had deep regrets. It was time I put her past behavior in perspective.

"Valerie, is there anything wrong with wanting love?" I asked.

"No. Of course not. We all need love," she replied.

"Does that include you?"

"Well, yes. It does. But what does that have to do with deciding whether I go back to school or open my own business?" she said.

"Everything. I don't want you to rush into a decision just because you are afraid of repeating the past. I want you to understand that the decisions you made in your twenties were not wrong."

"Not wrong?"

"Yes, not wrong. Not wrong for a woman looking for love and not knowing any other way to get it. You were just doing what you needed to do to get love. Traveling around the country wasn't stupid. It was your way to get your core need met. Your core need is to be loved." I assured Valerie that when we do things we regret it's because we are trying to get our core need satisfied. For her it meant drinking, giving up school, and traveling with a band. She didn't have the self-confidence or the knowledge to get her need for love met any other way.

We all have needs. Abraham Maslow created the Hierarchy of Needs Model. He discovered that our most basic needs must be satisfied before we can work on more emotional needs. His hierarchy of physiological needs includes air, water, nourishment, and sleep as the most fundamental. Once those are fulfilled, we can move up the ladder and go to the next level of needs, which are safety based. Do we live in a safe area, have job security, and financial reserves? The next level is social. We all need friends and a sense of belonging. The three first levels of needs already bring up challenging areas for some people. Imagine the difficulty you might have to get your more emotional needs met.

The final two levels of needs include esteem and self-actualization. When you have self-esteem, recognition, attention, and achievement, you can live by the tenets of self-actualization, including truth and wisdom.

From my brief description I hope you can gather that needs make up our primary motivation to take action. Valerie wanted love. She didn't know how to get it except to give up her own dreams and desires. It wasn't bad or wrong or stupid. It just was.

I want you to make Maslow's Hierarchy of Needs more personal. Look at the list below and ask yourself: What do I need to be content, satisfied, and fulfilled? What do I need above anything else to make sure I am okay? For some it might be love, while for others it might be safety. No core need is wrong. Go ahead and circle the five core needs you must have satisfied above anything else.

Core Needs

Respect	Safety	Fun	Space	Rest	Acceptance
Friendship	Openness	Honesty	Healthy	Support	Understanding
Family	Harmony	Trust	Commitment	Solitude	Faith
Fairness	Belonging	Love	Structure	Joy	Abundance
Power	Peace	Be Heard	Responsibility		Financial Stability
Success	Community	Change	Be Understood		Predictability
Be Included	Control	Express Feelings			

Now that you have circled your top five, please narrow it down to the three most important core needs. I understand it may be challenging to do, but I trust that you know what you need. Once you have your top three, go ahead and get it down to your top one core need.

Please write your number one core need: _____

Your core needs are the excuse behind your behaviors. Valerie's core need was love.

"Okay," I said. "Did you think you would be loved if you put men first?"

"Of course I did," Valerie chided. "But it didn't work."

Valerie was trying to get her core needs met. Every single person alive is just trying to get their core need met. If someone is rude to you, their core need may be control or space or to be heard. When someone is late all the time, their core need may be understanding or openness. Someone overcommitted to exercise may have a core need of health or predictability.

Valerie's core need was striving to be fulfilled but could only try based on the tools and skills she possessed. Making bad decisions was the effect. Her core need was the cause.

"Valerie, you just wanted to be loved. Is that so bad?" I asked.

Valerie looked up at me with tears in her eyes and whispered, "No." I assured her it was time to have compassion for herself for the decisions she had made in the past that were supposed failures. She had just been trying to get love the only way she knew how.

That was then, this is now. Valerie has learned many new skills, and if she found herself in the same situation now, she would handle it differently. Especially if she was aware that her core need was love.

Look through your past and tell me three situations that you wish hadn't happened.

1.
2.
3.

Ask yourself: How were you trying to get your core need met? When we are unaware of our core needs, they drive most of our decisions. When we become aware and can see our core need for what it is, an unfulfilled part of us that is fueled by our fears, we can make more thoughtful and empowering choices. It doesn't mean we still don't have the need, but we will be able to act on fulfilling it rather than reacting.

Until you are willing to be true to yourself, you will always look outside to satisfy your core need. You will wait for other people or situations to tell you you are okay. And you will always be disappointed. If you are proactive, and seek to satisfy and support your core need, you will have more courage to take the risks necessary to be your best you.

Letting go of your past regrets allows you to make powerful decisions in your present life. Regrets keep us stuck. They remind us of our failures and tell us to be cautious. Valerie had been living her life like that for over twenty years. She was ready to be free.

What actions will you take today to support your core need? For instance, instead of waiting for love to come to Valerie, I asked Valerie to be loving toward herself. That would satisfy her core need of love. She could get a massage once a week or take the time to walk around the lake with a friend or have her favorite soup for lunch. Little things that you do out of love for yourself add up. And those little things take away the desperation your core need might exhibit otherwise.

Another thing Valerie could focus on was the love she received from others. Rarely do we take it and accept it fully. I encouraged her to start accepting the love she is receiving rather than pushing it away.

When you understand that needs are a function of life, they will no longer make you feel bad or selfish or needy for having them. Discovering your specific needs gives you an opportunity to explore ways to get them met. Whether you learn more ways to self-love or ask others to support you, it is important that you learn to accept and honor your needs.

Today, Honor Your Core Need

Whatever your core need is, it is a pathway toward transformation. Your needs help you identify where you are lacking, where fear still lives within you. To support you in taking actions every day to fulfill your need, complete the following exercise.

Name five actions that would heal your core need:

1.
2.
3.
4.
5.

I asked Valerie to be loving toward herself. Can you do the same? Taking care of your own needs diminishes your insecurities and lessens regrets. What about ways your friends and family can satisfy your core need? Be open to creative ways for self-fulfillment.

I urge you to pay attention to your core needs throughout the day. Notice when you are not being true to yourself and connect it back to your core need. Being willing to honor your core need will support its satisfaction. If you ignore it, it will make itself known through inappropriate behavior and unpleasant feelings.

What could you do in the next twenty-four hours that could satisfy your core need and stop its hunger? Take at least three actions today that would help support your core need.

At the end of the day, be sure to write down the actions you took. Giving yourself credit is important to your self-esteem as you become more true to yourself.

1.
2.
3.

Day 12

Ask for What You Want

Sandra was Darlene's older sister. As the director of human resources for a small insurance company, Sandra was in charge of anything people related. Her experience came to good use dealing with her younger sister. Darlene was less responsible and would call Sandra several times a day to ask for help, share some news, or just complain. Sometimes Darlene would want a ride to the grocery store, even though it was within walking distance. Other times she would tell Sandra every single detail about her latest fight with a so-called friend. It was emotionally draining on Sandra, but she would always sigh and say, "She's my sister."

Until one week, when Sandra was diagnosed with pancreatic cancer and was scheduled for surgery six days later. When she told her sister, Darlene just moaned on about "what would she do" if something happen to Sandra. Obviously, anyone would be upset when they heard their sibling had cancer, but Sandra didn't need to hear how upset Darlene was. She needed support.

Sandra happened to attend a lecture I was giving to a local community group. As she listened to me talk about how I overcame my personal challenges, she decided to wait in line to meet me and ask for some advice. When it was her turn, she shared with me how her sister demanded to be first in their relationship and she kept repeating, "I have to confront Darlene."

Her friend Tammy stood by, nodding her head approvingly. When Sandra was finished, Tammy chimed in, "Yes, it is time for Sandra to confront Darlene. She doesn't have the energy to deal with her anymore. I told her to tell her sister, 'Support me or else.' What else is she going to do? It's not a good situation for Sandra anymore. She needs all the strength she can get."

"*Whoa!*" I said. "Let's slow down a bit. Okay, Sandra. Do you want a relationship with your sister?"

"Of course I do," Sandra exclaimed. "I just didn't know what to do. My sister is calling me every single day crying, asking me what is she going to do if something happens to me. I keep telling her nothing is going to happen but I have realized that's not the point. She has to be able to have a life with me or without me, and I need her to support me right now."

"I understand. But I just have a question. Have you told your sister what you want versus what you don't want?"

"What? What do you mean?" Sandra was clearly upset. "I have told her that I want her to quit calling me crying. And I have told her repeatedly that she can't ask for my help every day. But she just doesn't get it."

"Exactly. She doesn't get it because you aren't telling her what *to* do, you have been telling her what *not* to do," I explained. "Your sister sounds like someone who needs guidance in her life. Well, you can give her guidance and help her to become more independent all at the same time. You just have to change the way you speak to her."

Why do you tell the people you love what you don't want? If you tell me "Don't do this" and "Don't do that," I will most likely feel ashamed and insulted but hardly motivated to change. Focusing on the negative rarely works. It severs the connection between you and can hurt the other person's feelings. Depending on their temperament and maturity, they may call you names, become silent, or try to people-please. None of that is what you want.

When we tell the people we love what we want, they can help. Your friends and family will know what to do. They can contribute to you and feel like a part of the solution. Everyone wants to do the right thing. Giving your loved ones specific action steps supports them and supports you. They know what to do and you get your needs met. If you want to feel empowered and connected, give them a doable task and watch them perk up and listen.

The worst thing Sandra could do would be to focus on what she doesn't want. For instance, if Sandra tells Darlene to quit thinking about herself, Darlene will get more clingy, not less. Asking her to stop calling so often will only bring up Darlene's fear of rejection. Telling Darlene that she doesn't have the energy to deal with her any- more will trigger her anxiety about abandonment. Sandra can't avoid the issue by ignoring Darlene's calls. That will only fuel Darlene's fears. To solve the issue and heal the relationship you must be will- ing to ask for what you want and tell people what you need.

If you aren't willing to admit you need help, you are either a peo- ple pleaser, afraid to get rejected or look bossy, or feel that you are not worth the effort. All lies.

Sandra started to cry. "I just wanted her to quit draining me. I didn't know what else to say." I touched her shoulder and gently re- minded her that there is a solution.

I suggested to Sandra that she call Darlene and ask her to help but tell her exactly what she wanted and needed. The more concrete the better. If you aren't specific, you may not get what you want. Suppose you need some bread. You call up a friend and ask them to pick up a loaf, but you forget to tell them what kind. They don't ask, not be- cause they don't love you, but because they figure bread is bread. But it isn't and when they bring back whole wheat instead of rye, you get mad. It doesn't make sense but it happens all the time. People are getting upset or frustrated because they aren't satisfied with the re- sults they are getting. But the truth is, no one is telling anyone how to make them happy.

The more specific you can be, the more your wants and needs will be met. If it doesn't matter what kind of bread you get, give your sup- port team the freedom to buy the bread of their choice. But if that happens, you do give up the right to be upset. Be warned.

What did Sandra want from Darlene? It is important to get as clear as possible before you tell someone what you want. Sometimes it isn't easy to figure out. You might want to list anything and every- thing you "think" you want and then narrow it down. Being able to prioritize will help you focus on what matters most.

I asked Sandra to give me the top three things she wanted from her sister. Sandra wanted Darlene to:

1. Stay at the hospital with her before and after her surgery
2. Ask a friend to be in charge of Darlene's grocery shopping
3. Water Sandra's plants and feed the cat

"Sandra, are these doable for Darlene?" I asked.

"Yes. I believe Darlene can do all of those things; she just doesn't. I can't believe I am asking my sister to do something when she refuses to take care of herself."

"If you give Darlene a job to do, it will help her stay connected to you during your healing process. She will have a mission. We know she wants more of your attention because of her frequent calls. She probably doesn't think she can make a difference in your life. When you tell her what you want, you are giving your sister a gift. You are saying she can help you get better. That is so important. Can you imagine how you would feel if what you did actually helped someone?" I asked.

With Sandra's surgery only six days away it was time to take action. "Give her a call now," I urged. "Focus on one thing in this first conversation. What do you want the most from Darlene? And be sure to thank her for caring about you."

Tammy grabbed her phone and started to dial. "Here. Talk to Darlene. Rhonda's right. Darlene wants to help. She just doesn't know how."

"Hello." Darlene was now on the other end of the phone line.

I gave Sandra a nudge and whispered, "Go on and give it a try. What do you have to lose?"

I believe if you want someone to help you, you have to help them help you. By sharing what you want with the people who love you, you are doing just that. You are not just giving them hints and clues about what would make you happy. You are giving them concrete things to do that will make a difference in your life. When you do that, you are risking potential rejection. That is the pathway to intimacy. Being vulnerable means you may have to ask for help by being specific. Those are scary things for most people but necessary, if you want to be true to yourself.

I asked Sandra to stay focused on what she wanted. I reminded her that Darlene didn't know that Sandra was going treat her differently, and to give her a break if she didn't respond right away. It usually takes more than one try to get your point across. You have to be consistent in using your new skills in order for your friends, family, or coworkers to notice how you've changed. So she shouldn't get sidetracked by Darlene's comments.

This is what happened.

SANDRA: Darlene, I just wanted to call you and say thank you. Thank you for caring so much about me. By your calls I know you don't want anything to happen to me. That makes me feel good. I haven't told you that yet.

DARLENE: I don't want to be alone, Sandra. You have to get better.

SANDRA: I want to get better. And I need help. I need *your* help, Darlene. Are you willing to help me?

DARLENE: Yes, but I have to get some groceries first. Did I tell you about Harry? He is such a jerk . . .

SANDRA GENTLY INTERRUPTS: Darlene, thank you for trusting me with that story. You are so important to me. It would mean a lot to me if you would you come to the hospital and stay with me before and after my surgery.

DARLENE: Me? I don't know if I can. I have so much to do. I don't like hospitals.

SANDRA: I want you to be the last person I see before I have my surgery and the first person I see when I am in the recovery room.

DARLENE: I want to see you too. Okay. But I have to get groceries before I can do that. But I will. I will go to the hospital with you. Can I help you pick your pajamas?

The conversation was a success. Sandra kept the conversation focused on what she wanted. When Darlene strayed, Sandra gently brought her back and repeated her request. Another thing to note is Sandra might justly label Darlene's comment "I don't want to be alone" as selfish. But it is true. Darlene doesn't want to be alone. Learning to identify what triggers you—for instance, the words *selfish, stupid,* or *lazy*—will help you defuse your feelings fast when those words pop up in conversation. The end result: Darlene is helping Sandra.

Being willing to ask for what you want takes courage. And some people don't even know that they need something. One way to identify an unmet need is through your feelings. Sandra felt drained, exhausted, and frustrated—sure signs that she was expending more energy than she was receiving, proving that her needs were not being satisfied. Getting your needs met and asking for what you want will build your self-confidence and satisfy your soul, giving you the ability to share yourself without being depleted in the process.

Part of asking for what you want is being willing to go first. Jade didn't like to go first. She never asked a guy out but waited to be approached. It was safe. It had been five years since her divorce and she was no closer to finding the love of her life.

"How can you find the love of your life if you are sitting on the sidelines?" I asked.

"But I'm not aggressive. I am not that bold. Waiting for them to come to me reassures me that they like me," Jade said.

"Like you?" I replied. "They don't even know you. It sounds to me that you are afraid of being rejected."

Rejection is a common excuse. When most people feel rejected, it is because they are taking the rejection personally. If they don't get asked on a second date, they believe they did something wrong. If the person they are talking to leaves the party, they think it might be something they said. If you don't get invited to an event, you figure it must be you. What if none of that is true? Jade was about to find out that learning to deal with rejection builds confidence. Nothing brings up the fear of rejection faster than the thought of approaching someone first. But you must step forward and risk or you will never change your life.

"Apply this scenario to your entire life. Do you sit back and wait for a promotion? Do you secretly hope someone gives you a compliment? Do you wish that more people would ask you to their holiday parties? I am not saying that you have to approach every man you meet and ask him out. But are you willing to go for what you like, what you want?"

Jade thought that waiting for the man to ask her out was polite, proper, and ladylike. I assured her ladies ask. At least powerful ladies do.

"It sounds like you have an image of yourself that you would like to maintain," I said.

"I'm shy. And what's wrong with wanting to project yourself a certain way?"

"Once you become aware of your shyness, shyness becomes a choice. And there is nothing wrong with an image if it supports you, empowers you, and sets you free. In my mind a woman waiting by the phone does not fulfill any of those criteria. What if you meet a guy at a party, talk to him for a while, but he doesn't make a move? What do you do?"

"Well, I figure he isn't interested," she replied.

"But what if he is but he's shy, scared, nervous around you. What if *he* is afraid of rejection? Who is going to call first?"

Jade felt powerless to change her relationship situation because she believed that women who ask men out are considered loose or aggressive. She didn't want to be called either. Her fear of being judged was now deciding her fate.

But what could Jade do differently? How could she shift her mind-set? One way would be to set boundaries. When you have boundaries in place, you are free to risk because you know your limits. Being willing to go first means you can count on your boundaries to keep you safe. Let's say Jade approaches a man and he does call her loose. If she has determined that name calling is a boundary breaker, she knows it is unacceptable. She would walk away.

If you have boundaries in place, going first isn't so scary.

When you ask for what you want and are willing to go first, you are telling the world that you trust yourself. You know what you want and are confident that it has merit and worth. Other people's approval does not outweigh your own. Your boundaries matter to you because you matter to you.

Thinking about something is much easier than doing it. Jade was about to go first. At a fund-raiser for breast cancer she attended the evening after our session, she agreed to invite a man to the local coffee shop if she decided she wanted to get to know him better.

Cliff was a professor at the local college. He was at the event because his wife had died of breast cancer two years before. He was committed to obliterating the disease. He and Jade met because they were seated at the same table for dinner. His laughter was what got her attention. She wanted to get to know him better.

It took her almost three hours to gather the courage to go first. Jade was on the way back from the rest room when she saw him out of the corner of her eye grabbing his coat. It was now or never.

Putting her anxiety aside, she focused on what she wanted: a coffee date with Cliff.

Cliff and Jade have gone out on three dates and are getting to know each other. If Jade hadn't approached him, they would not be dating. Jade was his first date since he became a widower. It is taking courage for him to date again.

Sandra also got good results. Darlene did go to the hospital on the day of Sandra's surgery and did her best to be supportive. There may be times that Darlene wants to revert to complaining and whining to test Sandra's love, and Sandra can either revert back to her old ways of dealing with it and give Darlene a bunch of nos and don'ts or she can have compassion and stay focused on what she wants from the relationship.

I guarantee that when you help people help you by sharing what you do want, your needs and wants will be fulfilled with more ease than you ever imagined. People just don't know how to help and they feel stupid asking. Help them out and tell them what you want. You might be surprised at the results. And be sure to go first! And just like any conversation, be sure to be as compassionate and empowering as possible. It will yield better results.

Today, Ask for What You Want

Learning to identify how feelings and thoughts stop you from asking for what you want is vital to understanding why you haven't asked up until now. It is scary to ask for something without any guarantee of satisfactory results. But it is necessary for you to grow. Answer the following questions and be as thorough and truthful as possible.

Tell me about the last time you wanted something but didn't ask for it.

What stopped you from asking?

If you could ask for anything from anybody, what would it be and from whom?

How would your life change if you got what you wanted?

Can you see how your feelings and fears are holding you back? Can you see the benefit of fulfilling your needs and wants by asking for support? Everyone likes to help. I have yet to meet a person who doesn't raise his or her hand in agreement when I ask, "Who likes to help others?"

Noticing how much fear there is in your daily life, and how it manifests itself, will stop you from getting caught again. It is your day to ask for what you want. What do you need right now and how can your friends, family, and acquaintances help you get your needs met? You already know based on your answers above.

Commit right now to asking for what you want at least three times today. Make at least one a risk. If you are horrified when someone at your table returns food at a restaurant, perhaps that is someplace you can start. Have a nice lunch and be very specific about what you want. For instance, I like flavored iced tea. I am so addicted that plain iced tea just doesn't do it for me anymore. I have to add some juice to make it fruity. When the waitress takes my drink order, the first question out of my mouth is "What kind of iced tea do you have?" My sisters' eyes roll and they plead with me, "Can't you just order regular iced tea?" And I always answer the same, "No." If they only have plain iced tea I ask for what I want: "I would like an iced tea with a splash of cranberry, please." And you know what, I get what I want. You do the same. Take a risk today.

At the end of the day, please fill in the three ways you asked for what you wanted. Giving yourself credit is important if you want to continue to build momentum to change your life. Each time you write down something you did, you are proving to yourself that you can change.

1.
2.
3.

Take action today. Be true to yourself and speak up. Imagine the world wants to give you everything if you'd only go first and ask for it. Start asking and watch your dreams unfold.

Day 13

The Power of Words

At age twenty-three I was addicted to "I love you." I couldn't wait to hear my latest man whisper those three little words. Those words had the power to seduce me into changing the music I listened to and the clothes I wore. Since I wasn't sure who I was, I was like a chameleon with men. Tell me you love me and I will change anything.

Along with yearning to hear those three words I was the queen of "I don't care." I don't care what we do today. I don't care what movie we watch. I don't care what I eat. That phrase determined my relationships with people. Men had to take care of me. My friends had to decide everything. My work just tried to ignore me.

Using "I don't care" as my personal mantra was extremely disempowering for me. There were times when I tried to rationalize that "I don't care" meant I was evolved and therefore could be with anyone and deal with anything. I reasoned that I had surrendered my will for another's will. But that wasn't what Jesus had in mind when he said, "Thy will be done." He was talking about God, I applied it to everyone. My fear of rejection was so overpowering that I gave up my opinions to be liked by anyone. That is the power of words.

And how many times have you told a story and embellished just a bit to make the story better? Have you ever started to believe the lies you told? Your intention may have been innocent, perhaps you exaggerated for entertainment purposes, but it proves how our words influence us. The story you tell becomes fact and people share it with others as if it were true.

The words we use reveal our beliefs and shape our future. Most people don't think about how the words they speak define them. But they do. Just like "I don't care" became my personal mantra, you have your own. What words do you sprinkle in your conversations?

Circle the phrases that you use regularly.

It's hard . . .
I have difficulty . . .
I struggle with . . .
I gotta do it myself . . .
I can't afford . . .
You don't understand . . .
I sacrifice . . .
Don't worry about me . . .
I don't think I should . . .
I can get it all done . . .
If only I have more time . . .
No one can do it like me . . .
I can't . . .
No one works harder than me . . .
I am sorry . . .
You don't get it . . .
What is your problem?
I don't care . . .
You are such a . . .

The phrases you circled point to the reasons you are not being your best you. They make up your excuses and rationales. Words like *sacrifice, struggle, hard,* and *difficult* tell me that you let your feelings get the best of you. A deadline can come and go because you have a built-in explanation: You tried. It was just too hard. No one can blame you for failing after a gallant effort.

Phrases like "No one works harder," "Don't worry about me," and "No one can do it like me" are examples of self-defeating language. Martyrs also use the language of restriction and limitation. With the independent "I gotta do it myself" talk, there is little room for anyone to help you out because you have it all handled. But it can get lonely when you do everything yourself.

When your excuses are lack of money and too little time, you are held back by the material world. You are easily influenced and dissuaded from your goals. When you don't have enough time or money, people understand. Folks let you off the hook so you don't have to really go for your dream because in your own mind money and time are musts for success.

"You don't understand" is the ultimate put-down. It automatically puts people in their place. How can you have a conversation after that? How can anyone share their opinion? They were just told that they cannot contribute because they haven't experienced what you are going through. It reminds me of a conversation I had with a woman I will call Sue. Sue told me stories about how she felt left out at ballet class, was ridiculed by neighbors, and ignored by her schoolmates. She was African-American and told me that I could never understand what is was like to be black. I agree. I can't. But I have experienced the feelings of being left out, ridiculed, and ignored.

After my father murdered my mother, no one played with me from our community. I was labeled "one of those kids." Ignored by my own relatives and left to care for myself, I was ostracized, called names, and humiliated. Sue was from a wealthy, close-knit family. She never experienced working at the age of fourteen to pay her bills or being without a mother like I had. But I didn't doubt that she could understand me. I am sure she could. In her vast life experience I am sure she felt had felt loneliness like I had most of my life and in her own way I am sure she struggled. But that confirms the power of words. We used the same words to describe our feelings but because our experiences were different she believed I could not understand her. Maybe I am wrong, but I would hate to think that we can't understand each other well enough to connect even though we haven't lived the same life. I pray we can.

"I can't" and "I don't think I should" are the most common language blocks. Next time you are on the bus, in a café, or at a party, start listening to how many times you hear someone say *but* or *should*. It's an epidemic. And it affects our ability to be true to ourselves.

Janet attended one of my workshops. She was sitting in the front row, eager to learn. When I challenged the class to remove one excuse-ridden phrase from their vocabulary, Janet balked. She thought that there was no way it would have any impact. I asked her to be my guinea pig for the day. If she used any phrase that put her down, I would call it to her attention. She was up to the challenge.

Within the first hour I caught Janet sharing her thoughts, and it included the word *should*.

"I don't think I should have to work so hard to get ahead," she stated firmly. The group had been talking about their vision of success.

"Should?" I asked. "When you use the word *should,* Janet, it tells me you don't feel powerful enough or clear enough to state the truth, because, Janet, you don't *have* to do anything. After the age of eighteen everything is a choice. Could you reframe the question without the *should,* Janet?"

I could tell she was irritated with me but I wasn't interested in becoming her friend, I wanted her to become aware of how she disempowers herself over and over by using words that subtly put her down and keep her stuck. *Should* is one of the main culprits. *Should* keeps us focused on what other people want instead of what we want. I asked Janet to try again.

"I don't think I want to work so hard to get ahead." Janet was proud that she was able to exchange *should* for another word so quickly. But with her new word the statement had a new meaning and it revealed more truth that she wanted to attempt. The revelation? Janet didn't want to work hard.

During the next hour I caught Janet using the excuse "I can't afford to start my own business." It is a very seductive excuse because it is an excuse upheld and perpetuated by the media. You can hear your boss talk about the budget crunch and the president talking about a recession. Everyone is using a lack of money as an excuse.

"What if you didn't need money to attain your goal?" I inquired. She was getting annoyed with me. As always I asked her to reword her sentence. I told her to focus on other ways she could become successful. Money wasn't her only option.

"Money is only one of the resources I could use. Is that what you mean?" Janet quipped.

"Janet, my job is to point out how your words affect your state of mind. When you use the phrase 'I can't afford . . .' it implies that money is your only alternative. It tells me that you believe money is the answer to your problem. There are other ways to open a business. Be creative."

She bolted up in her seat when I caught her again within minutes when she said, "It's hard to open your own business." *Hard* is the wrong word to use if you want to empower yourself and change your life. I asked her to think of another way to say it. She finally came up with "There are challenges to overcome when you open your own business."

It may seem silly to put so much time and energy in to the words you use every day. But think of it this way: The words you use today create your future tomorrow. Do you want to leave that to chance?

Janet's language was perpetuating her fears. Her words reinforced that she is not to blame, it's not her fault that it's hard and she doesn't have the money. I can hear her already: "I work hard and it's tough to get ahead when you have bills to pay." Using that type of language keeps you stuck. It doesn't leave any room for creativity, ingenuity, and miracles.

I started my coaching career with a business card that I typed up on my computer. I used a business-card template and printed them on perforated business-card paper stock. It wasn't what I'd dreamed, but it was what I had. I used it for about six months before I had the resources to improve it. Notice I didn't say money. I didn't use money. I traded coaching sessions with a graphic designer for business cards and stationery.

When you change your language, you change your outlook. Eliminating the vocabulary at the beginning of this chapter is seemingly a small change, yet it will give you enormous results. Just think of how much your awareness will increase if you practice focusing on the words that come out of your mouth. Imagine how much more powerful you will feel when your words truly represent your best self. And what is truly empowering is you are ultimately in charge of what you say, when you say it, and how you say it.

I gave up the word *struggle* last year. I used to banter it around as if it were a shining medal of honor on my chest. Now I am working on *sacrifice*. I can get caught on all the things I had to go through to be where I am today. When I am fearless, I am eternally grateful but when I am in fear, I feel like I have to sacrifice.

The language you use also reveals your state of mind. Nothing will support you in shifting from fear to freedom quicker than your language. When you understand what language you use and when you use it, you will be able to catch yourself being fearful immediately. Language tells us so much about ourselves. If I hear myself say *should,* I know I am feeling obligated. When I hear the word *can't* come out of my mouth, I know I am feeling powerless. I use the word *whatever* when I am feeling like a victim; I am refusing to admit that I care about something I have no control over.

And you might not use the actual word but if it implies the same meaning, give it up. For example, I don't have to say the word *struggle* to make my point. I just have to tell you over and over again how hard I work and how little free time I have. A "sigh" usually follows. When I hear that sigh, I cringe because I was feeling sorry for myself. It is okay to have feelings, but to use them to manipulate another is where I draw the line between being empowering and disempowering.

At the risk of humiliating myself I am going to share some of the things I have said when fear was running my life.

I work harder than anyone else I know.
Sure, I have a television show, but you don't know what I had to give up.
I don't date. I don't have time.
You don't understand my schedule.
Vacation? I don't take vacations. I have to keep focused.
Are you kidding me? You want me to do what?
I will take a break in 2010.
I sure wish I could make your wedding (anniversary, birthday, retirement, etc.) party but I have to work. Have some fun for me.
A movie? I only have time to watch rented videos at three in the morning.
Oh, if I could only get a full night's sleep, but I have too much work to do.

My sense of struggle kept me focused on how I was giving and everyone else was taking. It wasn't true. I knew I was making it up, but I could barely stop myself because it had become so automatic. I had trained myself to value struggle over relaxation, happiness, or fun. I figured it would get me to heaven, but it only kept me up all night, made me resentful, and in turn, pushed people away. My struggle left me lonely.

I don't want the same thing to happen to you.

Cleaning up your vocabulary is essential to becoming a better you. Being vigilant about the words you speak is a great place to start. Go ahead and choose one of the phrases you circled at the beginning of this chapter. Now, for the next twenty-four hours, do not use that phrase. Eliminate it from your vocabulary. If you slip, and you might, just start again but extend the exercise another twenty-four hours. This isn't to punish you. It reinforces your commitment to change by letting go of any excuse. As always, no beating yourself up allowed.

Becoming aware of the words you use puts you in control. When you begin to correct yourself midsentence, that's the moment when you know you are integrating what you have learned. Be on the lookout. And be willing to change your language in the middle of a word. That is how you will become masterful at eliminating words that disempower you and implementing words that help you to be more you.

Your true self isn't afraid. Your true self wouldn't put you down. Your true self doesn't think money is the answer. Your true self isn't interested in how much time you do or do not have. Your true self makes choices. Your true self understands. Your true self includes others and wants to connect more than anything. Your true self empowers. Your true self relaxes, enjoys herself, and has fun. Be willing to be your true self.

Today, Let Go of Disempowering Language

Please list three of your most frequent words or phrases that keep you stuck. What do you say when your life gets difficult? What do you repeat when you think something is stupid, or silly, or a waste of time? Paying attention to the words and phrases you use will increase your awareness, thereby giving you more ability to change them.

1.
2.
3.

For the next twenty-four hours, eliminate those three words or phrases. If you slip, do not beat yourself up. This is an awareness-building exercise rather than one of perfection. Understanding what you can say instead is part of your growth. I want you to replace the words or phrases above with a word or phrase that empowers you and aligns with your intention.

List three options for replacements:

1.
2.
3.

Whenever you hear yourself say the words or phrases that disempower you, immediately replace them with these. It will feel awkward at times, that is understandable. Change isn't comfortable. The point is to do it regardless of how you are feeling. This is a true sign of mastery.

At the end of the day, please write down your experiences with eliminating words. It is imperative you keep a record of your change and transformation. Rarely do we reflect on who we have been and how we got to where we are. It is vital to honor your past. It brought you here.

Word elimination and replacement taught me:

Day 14

Liar, Liar

In order to move your life forward and be true to yourself, you must be willing to release all that is untrue. All the lies you have been telling yourself. The lies you have been telling others. Being willing to learn what is and what is not true is an important step in your journey to become a better you.

The challenge with lies is that we start to believe our own stories. Our perceptions turn into facts and we treat them as unchangeable. That is what lies do. They trick us into believing the good and bad exaggerated tales we tell ourselves.

How many people do you know who have a hard time accepting a compliment? When you don't believe a compliment, you are basically saying that the person is lying to you. Are they? What benefit is a compliment if you are not going to put any value on it?

I am not suggesting that you maliciously lie to yourself or to others. Most of the lies you tell are probably little white lies. Just like everyone else you rationalize that white lies don't hurt anyone. And if you didn't tell the white lie, the situation would become a hassle. Be blown out of proportion. It would become uncomfortable. It might get nasty. When you use a white lie as your defense, you are trying to convince yourself that it's for the best. It's as if white lies keep you out of trouble with the people in your life.

Derrick was always running late. He would make up little white lies about the weather or the traffic. Rarely would he admit that he had anything to do with it. It was always someone else's fault. He didn't want to look like a loser who couldn't get it together. Derrick's white lies affected his friendships and career.

White lies hurt you. Your integrity is damaged. Feelings are avoided. Real connection is missed. When you tell a white lie you are admitting that you are too afraid to deal with the situation. Maybe you don't think you can handle it or perhaps you think you shouldn't. When you tell a white lie you are giving up an opportunity to communicate with someone who matters. Intimacy is lost. Trust is nonexistent. Self-love is decreased.

It's one thing to say, "I'm sorry I'm late," but another when you say, "The traffic was terrible," when it wasn't. The first is an explanation while the second is a white lie. When you feel you must lie, you are telling the world you don't trust yourself to handle the situation. You are missing the chance to be true to yourself.

Learning to tell the difference between an explanation and a white lie is as simple as asking yourself: Is this an excuse? An excuse is usually exaggerated and a manipulated version of reality. Let's say there was traffic and that was the cause. Great, admit it. If there wasn't traffic but you were late because you left your house late, say you're sorry and move on. It's your feelings of guilt that tell you to lie.

What white lies do you lean on when a situation gets uncomfortable? Do you blame the traffic, your kids, work? Who is at fault if you don't show up on time? Every single time you feel you have to tell a white lie to avoid a sticky situation, you are reinforcing your fear of rejection. When you lie about something as simple as the traffic, I guarantee you are lying about more important things. Little lies point to big lies.

Derrick thought his white lies would help him skirt around any potential problems. When Derrick couldn't be forthcoming about his lateness, he was affirming that he was unreliable. No matter how he danced around the situation, his fear would come true: He would eventually be seen as someone who doesn't have it all together. No one likes to be lied to. No one likes to feel they were duped.

Victoria didn't want to hurt people's feelings. If she didn't think someone would appreciate something she did, she'd lie about it. People pleasers are chronic liars. They lie about what they want because they fear the truth would bring conflict. And to them, conflict is not good. White lies are the answer. An easy answer.

People pleasers lie because they think they have to. They are convinced no one will like them for who they are. Being true to themselves is the scariest thing of all. If you don't believe you have worth, why share your opinion? Her solution? Victoria needed to work on her self-esteem. Once she was able to see her own worth, people pleasing would cease and the lies that go with it.

How do you people-please? Is there someone in particular you have a hard time telling the truth to? Maybe it is your mother or husband? When you put someone else's needs above your own, you will pay for it by a decrease in self-esteem. All needs are equal. All wants are equal. All desires are equal. No one's love is worth your self-esteem. Honoring yourself will stop the lies of people-pleasing.

Exaggerating the situation was the norm for Laura. She thought her life as a bank teller was not exciting, so to make it more interesting she would embellish. Her husband didn't give her a dozen roses, he gave her two dozen. If she got a dollar raise she would tell everyone it was more. She told little white lies that didn't seem to hurt anyone but made Laura's life seem so much more exhilarating. Just like Victoria, Laura didn't see how her life was worth talking about because of her low self-confidence.

Everyone wants to feel important, and lying seems to turn imperfection into perfection and boring into exciting. For the moment. Lying will always perpetuate the fears behind it. Derrick, Victoria, and Laura all had the fear of being rejected. If they kept lying, that fear would become more real to them, not less.

Do you exaggerate? What are you afraid of feeling when you exaggerate? When I catch myself exaggerating, I can see that what I really want is to be heard. I want to make a difference, so if my story is just a little funnier, a little bigger, a little more than what it is, maybe I will be understood. It shows me that I still have insecurities about being good enough.

The same can go for people who don't even know they are lying, the ones who believe their lies. To them, their lies are truth. That is what happened to Jon. He had a horrible habit of making a joke when anyone complimented him or when he got uncomfortable or when he wanted to avoid his feelings. He laughed in order to push away his vulnerabilities and his fears.

Sheryl and Jon worked at a *Fortune* 100 company. Together they had developed software that would simplify the data entry process. It was hailed by their boss as the next big thing. After testing was com-

pleted and its abilities confirmed, Jon and Sheryl were informed that
as a way of the company saying, "Good work," there would a monetary bonus in their next paycheck.

Sheryl was enjoying the kudos her collegues were giving her. Her
bonus money was going to be put to good use. She was going to Ger-
many with her son to visit the grandmother she had never met.

Jon, on the other hand, was making sure his friends were laughing with him as he told his story of woe; how he developed this software program with no help from Sheryl, his job was going nowhere,
and he wasn't feeling supported. That is the story he was telling me
during our first coaching session together, when I cut him off and
asked him what was so funny. He let out a laugh and told me he was
just thinking about what a joke it would be if he quit his job.

Throughout our hour conversation he probably said three serious
things. If he could admit three things, I knew eventually he would get
to the truth. In reality he might have a flair for humor but he was
using it to avoid his heart, head, and soul. Telling the truth was difficult for Jon because he believed that if he said what he really felt,
something bad was going to happen. He was so afraid of being rejected and seeing people laugh at him, why not turn the tables and
make them laugh first? He would win. He wouldn't dare allow himself to believe that people could actually like him for him. His jokes
were driving a wedge between him and any meaningful friendships.

Jon was afraid of the truth.

Jon admitted that he wanted people to like him and he thrived on
people's laughter. That's fine but they weren't laughing with him, they
were laughing, with some discomfort, at him. Who really feels good at
someone making a joke that is sarcastic and somewhat cruel? Jon
only heard the laughter. He didn't want to think about why they were
laughing.

I brought this to his attention. "Jon, do you think you are liked for
being you?"

"I don't know. I am naturally funny. I've always been told that. So
I don't see what the problem is. I came to you for coaching to find
love, not to quit making jokes," Jon said.

"Yes, Jon. I understand," I replied. "But what if your jokes are the
reason you are alone? Have you ever thought that your jokes might
push people away?"

I helped Jon to see that when he made a joke about everything and anything, he wasn't sharing his truth. The jokes were a substitute for true connection. He was lying about his feelings. He was lying about who he was. Jon was caring and sensitive and funny. But all anyone saw was Jon trying to push away his feelings and avoid serious conversations by deflecting everything with laughter. It was painful to laugh with Jon, because it wasn't always funny.

We tell lies to save ourselves from asking for help or saying we are sorry or admitting we need love. We tell lies so we won't put anyone on the spot or hurt another's feelings. We tell lies in order to ensure we will be loved. We tell lies to avoid our own pain, our own yearnings, our own broken heart.

Jon used jokes to reveal his feelings in a way he could deny later on. "What do you mean I said I was upset? It was a joke!" he would say if anyone cornered him. And what could they say? He left people with no opening to get close. He was alone and the jokes made him lonelier.

I asked Jon to make a list of all the situations he wanted to avoid over the next twenty-four hours. That would be the time his joke telling would be at full force. Think about what you do to hide the truth from yourself and others. Do you cook when you don't want to feel? Do you clean, take a drive, focus on the garden? What do you do to avoid telling the truth about who you are? Maybe you get tired or go for a run. What situations are you trying to avoid in your own life?

I am not talking about healthy outlets such as taking a time out to get your thoughts in order and your feelings understood. I am talking about avoiding, denying, and hiding and never sharing any feeling or thought with anyone.

And I am not asking you to start confessing every single feeling and thought you have. That would be inappropriate. What I do care about is when you are avoiding the truth. When you are avoiding the truth, you are avoiding being vulnerable. You are failing to experience intimacy.

List five situations where you have avoided telling the truth:

1.
2.
3.

4.

5.

What did you do to avoid or deny the situation? Smile? Walk away? Blame someone? Cry? Get angry? Make a joke?

1.

2.

3.

4.

5.

Congratulations! You have told the truth. I know it is scary to reveal your pathway of avoidance, but consider it as moving one step closer to your true self.

For the next six months Jon worked diligently on truth telling. He still had his sense of humor, but he quit using it to avert the situations that were difficult. Understanding the difference between using laughter to lie and using laughter for enjoyment was a big step for Jon. But he eventually became successful at it. Today Jon has a new hobby. He is a stand-up comic at night and develops software during the day. And recently he starting dating Diana.

I think by and large most people try to be honest. We admit we are late or confess to little white lies. But some people are too honest. Barb was notorious for her honesty. When Barb didn't like something, she told you. Whether it was your clothes, hair, or boyfriend, nothing was off limits. Her favorite line was: I am just telling the truth. Barb didn't come to see me. Her husband did. Gerald couldn't take it anymore. Barb had turned telling the truth into something destructive.

Gerald wasn't the only target. Barb would call up their daughter Cindy and give her unsolicited advice on dating. Barb always had something to say. Things like "Honestly, Cindy. He isn't right for you. Did you notice that he was five minutes late for dinner? That is so disrespectful. You have to dump him! And by the way, you look tired, Cindy. This relationship is obviously affecting your health. I just want to be honest with you. After all, I am your mother."

And of course, Barb had to tell Gerald all about it under the guise of honesty. Being honest does not mean you share every single thought or feeling, but it did to Barb. Her entire family was exhausted and Cindy was being suffocated by her mother's love of honesty.

I told Gerald he had to be the role model for Cindy. I coached Gerald to repeat, "Thank you for your thoughts," anytime Barb was "honest" with him. And this was the hard part: Do not take Barb's comments personally. The payoff for Barb came when he reacted. If he didn't react, she wouldn't feel it necessary to tell the truth.

If she continued badgering him with her honesty, I told him to quietly and kindly say: "Thank you for caring about me." When someone is bugging you, they are unconsciously asking for attention and validation. Acknowledging their efforts will help them feel satisfied and move on from the situation.

I shared with Gerald one more step. If she still didn't stop, he would have to become firm and tell her: "Your truth is not my truth. I respect yours and I am asking you to respect mine."

It was very difficult for Gerald to follow my instructions. Barb was his wife and he loved her, but her honesty act was getting in the way of their marriage. He had to take a stand or he would continue to feel degraded by her "I'm just trying to be honest" line.

Barb is a classic case of using honesty to avoid the truth. It isn't any of her business what Gerald wears or who her daughter dates. But Barb uses honesty to be in control of every situation. If Gerald and Cindy would put boundaries in place and stick to them, Barb might learn how to share her feelings and thoughts only when asked. It wouldn't be dishonest to hold back. It truth, it would be respectful of someone else's wishes, wants, and desires.

Do you have someone in your life who is "just being honest" without being asked? Say, "Thank you for caring," and change the subject. If they don't get the hint, take the steps that I asked Gerald to take. Your individuality needs to be honored, not destroyed by another's "honest" opinions.

When you are willing to confess up to your lies, real intimacy can be cultivated. Lies help you deny that you are scared. But you are. When you admit it, others can support you. You will feel loved. That's another thing about lying. It doesn't let the love in.

Pay attention to when you lie, who you lie to, and the reason behind the lie. When you begin to separate the facts from fiction, you will be able to discern lies from truth, which will help you trust yourself. That's what lies take away. If you listen, they take away your ability to trust yourself. Your potential will be unfulfilled because lies stunt your growth. I encourage you: Keep growing. Be willing to share your truth.

Today, Do Not Lie

We all lie. Not intentionally the majority of the time, but sometimes we do to make the situation easier. In the moment, we are not counting the cost to our integrity and self-esteem. We are usually using another's feelings as our excuse, our justification to lie. We lie when we are being less than our best. Facing that you do lie is important if you are going to lay claim to your true self.

Name three white lies you use frequently.

Who are you protecting with your lies?

If you didn't lie, what do you think would happen to your relationship?

What do your lies say about you?

Coming to grips with your desire to lie will help you decide who you want to be. Do you want to be someone who defends and protects everyone with her lies? If yes, do you think it makes you a better person? Being true to yourself includes being truthful about the lies that systematically tear apart your confidence. Lies feed your fears. Do not let your fears win today.

Today is No Lie Zone. For the next twenty-four hours no lie shall be uttered from your lips. Not even something small like "I have to go to the bathroom" if you don't. Any lie is a lie. No more small or big or white lies. I am not asking you to share everything with every-one. That is not what I am requesting. Remember, just because some-one wants you to tell them something doesn't mean you have to. Don't lie about it, instead say, "Thank you for asking but that's pri-vate." When you refuse to lie, you are refusing to sacrifice yourself for the sake of others.

At the end of the day, please list the three most pivotal moments you had today. Keeping a list of your accomplishments will help you keep growing.

1.
2.
3.

Congratulations! You have proven to yourself that lies do not de-fine you. Being true to yourself means having integrity. Keep it up.

Day 15

Trusting Heart

When I was growing up, I trusted my parents to take care of me. When I got married, I trusted that my husband's love would last a lifetime.

My parents' deaths left me an orphan and my husband divorced me. My trusting heart was broken.

What is trust? How does one begin trusting again? How do we trust at all?

As a child I trusted people implicitly. I didn't *decide* to trust, I just did. I talked to anyone, shared stories with strangers, and made everyone my best friend. As we get older (or more cynical), the feeling of trust is not as easily achieved.

What is trust? Trust is the ability to have faith in someone's words and deeds. Maybe even in their mood. Consistency in telling the truth and keeping your word are imperative in building trust. I trust people. I trust people to be human. I trust humanity. And humanity is not perfect.

And what about trusting yourself? I know few people who can count on themselves to keep a promise. How many times have you said you are going to cut out the sweets, walk a mile a day, and actually do it? We want others to be trustworthy, yet we rarely are to ourselves.

What does trust mean to you?

I think most people equate trust with fulfilled expectations and loyalty. I know I did. I had expectations that my husband would never leave me. I definitely had expectations that my parents wouldn't die, leaving me to raise myself. I think we throw the word *trust* around to

test if people care about us . . . enough! It isn't any one person's responsibility to make sure all of your needs are taken care of. The
only person in charge of that is you. Why would you trust others to
think of you first when you can't even do that for yourself? I have
learned that you can trust others, yet it starts with trusting yourself.
And part of that is understanding that everyone is not going to follow
through on everything they say, because no one is perfect.

Pay attention to what I said about "trust" and "testing." How often
do you hear folks scream out in rage, "I don't trust you!" I want to interrupt and say, "I think you mean you don't trust you." In order to
trust others you must first trust yourself. Trust your own thoughts,
feelings, and actions.

Brenda wanted to break up with her boyfriend of six months. She
knew their relationship wasn't going to work, but whenever she told
him never to call her again, he would change her mind. Brenda did
not trust herself. One day Brenda will once again claim she can't trust
him but will she ever realize that her problem is that she doesn't trust
herself?

Lee was determined to change careers. He wanted to be a wrangler
in the rodeo, but his brother told him it was a dumb career move. He
would never make any money and just get beat up trying. Lee never
became a cowboy. He trusted his brother's opinion over his own.

Patty wanted to go out to New York to study art. She had been accepted to New York University and was in the process of finding hous-
ing. Her mother was upset that Patty had chosen NYU over Virginia
Tech. Going to Virginia Tech had been a tradition in their family for
generations. And now, according to her mother, Patty was turning her
back on her family. Her mother said, "If I can't trust you to make a
simple decision like this, how can I trust you with your inheritance?"

We use the word *trust* to manipulate others while avoiding trusting ourselves. That's what Patty's mother did. She used "I don't trust
you" as a device to get Patty to do what she wanted. The same goes
for Brenda. When she didn't trust her boyfriend, she used that
against him even though she had a hand in the problem. Brenda
didn't trust herself, but then blamed her boyfriend for hurting her.
When you find yourself spitting out the words "I don't trust you,"
please look in the mirror and ask if you're being true to yourself. The
answer most likely will be no.

And highly charged encounters are not the place to practice trust-ing another. When we are building our trust muscle, we need to start small and expand. In critical situations, such as a hospital stay or emergency, we can forget our fears and create trust instantaneously based on referral or reputation. We want to trust, we need to trust, so we do. Caution: Always put more weight on your intuition versus another's recommendation.

Trust is built one conversation at a time, one encounter at a time. There are levels of trust. I can trust you to feed my cat, yet I may not trust you to be faithful to me. That's why it is important to reveal our-selves in layers when we meet someone new.

First, we talk about the "safe" subjects. We bond over the mundane: our complaints and shallow topics that often preclude any deep shar-ing. For instance, talking about what dentist you use or bragging about your dry cleaner are safe subjects to bond over. Finding common ground is a great way to build trust.

Embryonic conversations for Brenda would include starting to make friends outside of her boyfriend. Having other influences would help her gain self-trust. The same goes for Lee. I would ask him to thank his brother for his advice but move on to folks who are living their dreams. A safe step would be attending a workshop or seminar and discussing how to fulfill a dream. If Patty wants to become an artist, trust is critical to the creative process as well as being a com-ponent of healthy self-esteem. Joining an artist group might be a first step to help her start seeing the difference between herself and oth-ers. No opinion is wrong when it comes to art, but your own opinion needs to matter.

List three people you trust on this level. You can rely on them to provide good safe conversation.

1.
2.
3.

Next, we begin exposing ourselves. We share more personal stories that reveal more of what we believe, our opinions and our dreams. To do damage control we become sensitive to other persons' reactions. Depending on our ability to trust ourselves we may be tempted to analyze their every move. If we feel secure or understood or heard, we may keep upping the ante. We share more and more of who we are as trust expands.

For Brenda it would mean talking to someone about relationships who would understand how difficult it is to leave. Lee could gain a mentor, a successful rodeo rider, to help him trust his decision. Going to NYU and meeting with other students would support Patty in understanding if NYU was the school for her. When we are willing to venture out of our safe, secure comfort zone, we begin to believe in who we are and what we stand for. We must trust ourselves if we are ever going to be happy with our success.

Whom do you trust to expose another layer of you? Whom do you share your stories with? Whom do you ask for help? List three people worthy of your trust.

1.
2.
3.

Lastly, we become vulnerable. We are willing to get angry, be hurt, and feel uncomfortable. This level of trust is what we all want but few have experienced. This is where true intimacy is created. It is where unpleasant things are said, misunderstandings happen, and heartbreak occurs. But we stay and work it out. We know the hurtful things were done out of fear. We look beyond the words and focus on what was the purpose behind it. We ignore tone and style and only hear what was meant to be said. This is where trusting ourselves proves to be the key to love. It is the place we must be willing to go if we want to trust ourselves in order to trust another.

If Brenda is going to break up with her man for good, she must be at this level of trust within herself. Lee needs to know that love is more than agreement. When you truly trust yourself, you are willing to go through the uncomfortable feelings of not getting along. Telling his brother he loves him, but that he is going for his dreams, means Lee has learned to trust himself. Patty must stand up for herself. And learn to trust herself implicitly. When others try to manipulate us we must first become aware of what is happening, and then trust ourselves more than the other. In this situation, putting our own insights first guarantees that we trust our intuition.

I can name a few people I trust at this level. The deciding factor is I do not feel judged no matter what I do. If I say something stupid or act foolishly or do something idiotic, they still love, respect, and care for me. I place my trust in people who don't take things personally and don't get caught in my mood. Folks like that are invaluable to me and when I find people like that, I want them in my life.

This last level is the hardest because so few of us are willing to expose all of ourselves. We must be vulnerable first before we can ask others to share themselves with us. Whom have you become vulnerable with and now trust them to see your heart?

1.

2.

3.

When we are true to ourselves, trusting others is easy. We can count on ourselves to say no when we need to and yes when it is appropriate. There is no second-guessing. No doubt. No waiting for proof.

But what about the people we love who let us down or "betray us"? And what about when we let ourselves down time and time again?

Who has betrayed your trust? List three people who have let you down.

1.

2.

3.

A characteristic of a trusting heart is the knowledge that no one is perfect, including you. Therefore, there is no beating up another for his or her failures. No punishment to earn back your love. No testing to see if they deserve a second chance. There can be no trust when perfection is your goal. Perfectionism takes away all ability to trust.

When someone breaks our trust, we must ask ourselves if we contributed. Were we awake in the relationship? If the answer is no, we have some learning to do. Putting boundaries in place, being present in the relationship, being willing to see and speak the truth. If the answer is yes to being present and the trust was broken, there is healing work to do.

My dear friend Marta and I had a huge fight last year. She was helping me run the coaching program for the Fearless Living Institute by sharing her wisdom with the new coaches starting the training process. We had always had a pact that friendship would come before business. But one day that failed. Our conversation turned cold when she wouldn't quit talking to me about business when I needed her love, not her advice. I needed my friend, not a coach. In my eyes my friend had betrayed me. It appeared to me that work was more important than my heart.

When we had our disagreement, I needed her to support me. When she didn't, I lost trust in her ability to be my friend. I can talk to anyone about my life's work but my personal feelings are sacred. I wanted them to be honored. I just forgot to tell her that. We had been friends for so long, I assumed she knew.

We didn't talk for weeks, and months later finally made up. It seems silly now, but at the time I was devastated. Marta was one of my most trusting relationships and when we had our falling-out I was forced to learn how human even best friends can be.

Never deny the love you had. Never act as if it didn't exist or wasn't real. It was. Love doesn't guarantee that there will always be trust between you. People get afraid and they do things that do not represent their best. People lash out when they don't know what else to do. People hurt other people because they are hurting inside.

We must be willing to forgive. Forgiveness is necessary in mending broken trust. First and foremost we must forgive ourselves for thinking anyone, ourselves included, could be perfect and live up to our expectations. We must forgive for trusting another over ourselves. Maybe in the beginning they were someone we thought we could trust, but over time, situations changed. Maybe we chose to ignore the signs because we didn't want to shift the relationship status. Maybe they changed and we wanted them to stay the same. Forgiveness is integral to our ability to trust again.

Who must you forgive in order to trust again?

I am going to delve deeper into forgiveness in Day Nineteen. Today, I want you to focus on what trust means to you. When you start to have a personal experience of what it means to trust yourself, it will be ten times easier to be true to you.

I trusted my husband and my parents more than myself. If you trust others *more* than yourself, the relationship is primed to become codependent, based in need versus want. When we repeatedly let ourselves down, that is a sign that we don't trust our own thoughts, opinions, or feelings. Maybe we don't even trust the values we stand for. In that instance we give away our power, making other people's opinions more important than our own. Self-trust is then hampered. Forgiveness is necessary to move past the hurt and build self-trust.

I remember the moment I got the value of trusting myself. I was dating Shawn and things weren't going well. He had told me I was needy and I guess I agreed. I was feeling unhappy. I thought, maybe I was just too demanding.

Before I got together with Shawn that evening I called Marta to get it off my chest. As I told her about my frustrations and fears, I admitted that I did feel needy. And then she said something that I still remember to this day. It had a profound impact on my life and still does. She said, "If you are needy, he isn't fulfilling your needs." WHAT?

You mean it isn't always my fault? I am not the needy person who can never be fulfilled? You mean, he might not be the one? Are you saying that if I have unmet needs, it might not be the relationship for me? I have learned to fulfill my own needs. I am the queen of taking care of myself, but a relationship also offers an opportunity to share my needs with another. I wanted to pinch myself. For my entire life I had been labeled overly sensitive. It was always my fault if my needs weren't being addressed because it seemed I had too many.

When I started to trust who I was and gain confidence, my needs were no longer overwhelming. I didn't feel like I was a drain on my relationships anymore. But with Shawn my insecurities were surfacing again. It must be me, I thought. Here we go again. What is wrong with me?

When Marta told me that Shawn had a responsibility to honor my needs because of our commitment, I wanted to jump and holler. A light bulb went off inside my head that has stayed lit ever since. When I feel needy, I am not trusting who I am. I am wanting outside confirmation. At that moment I think I need that validation from someone else to be okay. I am not trusting my path, my mind, or my heart. I am not trusting that my soul is on a journey of self-discovery. I was trusting Shawn's version of me rather than my own. When he told me I was too needy, I believed him. I had quit trusting me.

Learning that aspect of trust was revolutionary to me. Knowing that trusting myself was the key to having trust in any other relationship was significant to me. It changed my life and gave me an opportunity to trust who I was on a deeper level. When I value my opinions, beliefs, and thoughts I am being true to who I am.

If you hesitate trusting another, I am not saying dive in. Follow the three levels of trust to determine what is appropriate for your current state of relationship. Each person must be evaluated by their own merit. Valuing integrity over feelings and deeds over words will support you in trusting others.

How many times have you withheld trust and missed an opportunity? Trust is fragile. It must be nurtured, honored, and respected. And I choose to err on the side of trusting more, rather than less. I want to risk getting hurt for the potential feeling of love. I want to trust another until I am given a clear-cut reason not to. After my divorce I knew I was on the road to healing when I began to trust again. I gave up blaming myself and instead forgave my husband, as well as myself. In that moment I was free to trust.

Can you trust yourself to listen to your heart and think with your head? Can you trust yourself to follow through on your commitments and promises? Do you trust your intuition, the knower within? Learning to trust your own truth is vital to trusting others. I want to count on me. I want to trust that I will take care of myself first, and then expand that trust outward. I want to trust my intuition and walk confidently toward my dreams.

Trust is a main ingredient to peace of mind. Trust is sacred. Honor your inner voice. Listen. Trust happens when you are true to yourself.

Day of Trust

Without trust peace of mind is not possible. Be willing to trust yourself today. Imagine putting value on your opinions over another's or saying your thoughts first.

How would your life be different if you trusted yourself?

What is your criteria for trusting another? What actions do they take that garner your trust? For example: Do they call when they say they will? Do they follow through when a promise is made?

Make a list of people who are in your life but whom you don't trust.

What is it about them or their behavior that makes you hesitate? Seeing red flags is vital for discerning whom to trust.

Today, practice trusting yourself:

List any moment of potential trust you have with yourself or another. Rate yourself on a scale of 1 through 5, according to your ability to trust in that moment (5 indicating the highest level of trust). Pay attention to whether feelings or behavior dictate trust.

Discovering your criteria for trust will help you in discerning whom to trust or how to help others learn how to be trusted. The most important person for you to trust is yourself. You cannot possibly be true to yourself without the element of self-trust. Understanding how you determine it or disengage from it will help you stay true to yourself.

Day 16

The Myth of Balance

I don't know anyone who isn't busy. Whether working in an office, out in the field, or staying at home, we are being pushed and pulled by the rapid pace of society more than ever. We are overwhelmed with magazines, newspapers, bills, cards, direct marketing mail, and the latest invention, e-mail, all screaming, *Read me.* We are being engulfed by the information age. There is so much to see, do, and become, it can be exhausting as well as confusing. And the remedy, we are told, is balance.

Maureen wanted more balance. She had three kids under the age of seven and a husband who traveled for work. Besides being a wife and mother Maureen was part owner of a temporary employment agency. She was beat.

Her day started at 5:30 A.M. when she rolled out of bed. Every morning she threw on her sweats and gym shoes to walk two miles before the kids got up. By 6:45 A.M. she was showered, dressed, and cooking breakfast. Her three-year-old, Hannah, was always up by 7:00 A.M., and by 7:15 everyone else was vying for her attention. Between getting Jeremiah ready for first grade and Sarah for kindergarten, Maureen would be washing clothes and playing hide-and-seek with Hannah.

When her husband, Todd, was home, he added another element. He would turn on the television to watch CNN, and invariably Jeremiah would be sitting in his father's lap. Of course Maureen wanted them to spend time together, but not in the morning. It always put her behind. And she would get angry at the two of them for her failed morning. It was almost easier when he wasn't home to get her day going, and that made her feel guilty. In response, Maureen would commit to working harder to find more balance in her life.

It was clear to me that Maureen was putting a lot of pressure on herself to find balance. That perfect magical place where time seems to stand still and work, play, and love are all equally honored. Because as she says, "I know it is the answer to my problems."

I have found that many people create a lot of stress in their lives in their quest to have the perfect balance. We are afraid if we don't do the proper amount of self-nurturing, along with eating healthy, and with working enough but not too much, we aren't using our full potential. If we could just find the perfect combination to our lives, everything would surely fall into place.

When I ask people to define what they mean by *balance* they usually blurt out something about balancing home with work or spirit with materialism. They include words like *ease* and *regularly*. What about you? What is your definition of balance?

Define *balance:*

If you had a balanced life, how would it look?

I told Maureen that balance is nice in theory, but how do you stay balanced when the only thing constant in the world is change? And that's the good news. Change means we are risking and stretching past our limited beliefs.

Maureen understood that change was good, but she still yearned for balance. "Can't I just maintain going to the gym regularly or eating veggies every day? It seems like those things are the first to go when I am stressed out. Balance is so elusive." She sighed.

Balance is hard to pin down if you are using the outside world to determine it. I mean, sometimes it's appropriate to work overtime, while other times it wouldn't be. If you rigidly tell yourself that forty hours a week is the correct balanced amount, you might be cutting yourself off from potential opportunities that may not occur from nine to five. And there will be times when your family will come first before that project deadline. And only you know what would align with your long-term versus short-term commitments.

Maureen admitted that she felt guilty. She thought that seeking balance was the best thing for her family, but she was realizing there wasn't enough free time, i.e., hours with no scheduled activities. I encouraged her to redefine *balance*. Balance emanating from the inside is the balance I seek. The balance within is knowing you can recover from your hurts, moods, and frustrations easier than before. It is that knowingness that no feeling lasts forever. Do you have peace of mind? How fast are you able to realize you are acting inappropriately and get back to center? Can you shift from your head to your heart with ease?

People who seek the perfect balanced lifestyle are people who want things to manifest without fail. If you are addicted to perfection, I invite you to pay attention to your desire for balance. It might be just the enlightened way to be perfect. If your need for balance is being created by a drive to compete with the neighbors, it is being nurtured by your fears. Be attentive. Your motivation determines your results.

There is a simple solution to help you attain balance from within. Give up seeking balance based on outside criteria. Instead, focus on living a life devoted to internal balance. Being able to quiet your mind, make decisions, and recover quickly from loss are guideposts. If you concentrate and follow through on what you are committed to, if your commitments are based in freedom, balance will work itself out. Commitments are the solution to balance.

Think of three commitments that would support you in being more true to yourself. Would it be telling the truth without exception, living a healthy lifestyle, or giving up complaining? Commitments vary from person to person. I encourage you to pick three that could make a radical impact on your life.

To help you, here is a list of several different areas of your life where commitments may be found. They include: health, career, love, friendship, family, creativity, play, leadership, money mastery, time, and support. Feel free to think of your own.

What are your three top commitments?

1.
2.
3.

If you want to know what you are committed to, look at how you spend your time. You will soon see what life you have been committed to living.

Let's break it down some more. Who are you committed to? List the top five people in your life. Ask yourself: Do you spend enough quality time together? Is your relationship where you would like it to be?

1.
2.
3.
4.
5.

Commitments end up suffering without people who care about you. It is impossible to work twenty-four hours a day without support and love. It is a waste of time to do work on balance unless you are aware of who you want to include in your downtime.

Now, let's get really specific. Since we are talking about balance, please tell me how much time each commitment could take each week.

Commitment 1:
Commitment 2:
Commitment 3:

What is the reality of keeping that schedule over the next three months?

If the time spent is ignored, how do you plan on evaluating whether your commitments are valued?

Each of us has a process we go through that determines what makes something valuable. It may be the time you put in or the money or the effort. What determines value to you? Having that answer will help you discover why certain commitments are easier to keep. For instance, Maureen kept track of commitments by time. Her time was more valuable to her than money. If she spent time, it meant something to her.

To shift from an external focus, Maureen had to determine why she gave one thing more time versus another. I wanted Maureen to look at all her goals, desires, and wants to find a common thread. When you have something in common in every situation, it is easier to be committed and stay centered.

Think of commitments as your decision-making criteria. If you are committed to family, working overtime must be weighed against the effects it will have at home. And if work is exciting and creative, the responsibilities of manifesting your dream must be weighed daily against how it affects you socially as well as in your intimate relationships. Your commitments might include becoming a more loving person, living a healthy lifestyle, or working with a mentality of excellence. Or they could be more basic: love your job, have good friends, and spend time with your children.

I asked Maureen to name her top three commitments as well as look at her schedule to see how much time she was devoting to each. Her sigh gave it all away. When commitments do not dictate your time schedule, your priorities can fall by the wayside and decisions can be determined by life's emergencies. No wonder few people feel balanced. Keep track of your activities today. How you spend your time and the attitude you exhibit while doing them is going to tell you what commitments you are living by now. Just like Maureen, you may or may not like it.

Do I want you to have more fun, work hard, and love more fully? Yes! Do I want you to be energized as well as be a relaxation specialist? Yes! I want you to feel alive, and sometimes that will mean sleeping a little or a lot. It could mean working sixty hours a week or it might mean getting home at five o'clock on the dot. Things will always change in your life, but when you use commitments as your guiding force you will access your true self time and time again.

Maureen wanted to stay true to her commitments—but she had to reevaluate what she wanted to really commit to. She chose three: be kind to herself, spend time daily with her children on an individual basis, and excel at work. She loved her job, and since she was part owner she had the flexibility needed to stay focused on her top three commitments.

Being true to your commitments guarantees you will have internal balance. As you live a life that you create, you will feel more powerful and courageous. Therefore, you will start to feel that your life is your own. It's up to you. I encourage you to give up the word *balance* and substitute the word *commitment*. Your life will be filled with more self-love. Your choices will be aligned with your values. Decisions will be easier to make. Life will naturally include more peace of mind and personal satisfaction. You will effortlessly be more true to yourself.

Today, Live by Commitments

When you look at your life it is evident what your commitments are. If balance has been valued, I urge you to focus on your commitments as the means to accomplish your goal of balance. Please answer the questions below. When you discover what internal factors support you externally, your life will get simpler and therefore easier. Who doesn't want to have more ease in their life? Stay open!

1. Do you live by your commitments now?

2. Are you happy with your commitments?

3. What is the difference between a life driven by balance versus commitments?

4. If you could have balance in one area of your life, what would it be?

For the next twenty-four hours, look at your life through the eyes of your commitments. Pay attention to your mood and your attitude as you shift your focus from balance to what you are committed to. Fill out the twenty-four-hour Life Log. Write down everything you do. Looking at how you spend your time gives you the reality check you need to change it.

Today's Life Log

Keep track of your activities to determine your present commitments.

TIMES	Today
6:00 A.M.	
7:00 A.M.	
8:00 A.M.	
9:00 A.M.	
10:00 A.M.	
11:00 A.M.	
Noon	
1:00 P.M.	
2:00 P.M.	
3:00 P.M.	
4:00 P.M.	
5:00 P.M.	
6:00 P.M.	
7:00 P.M.	
8:00 P.M.	
9:00 P.M.	
10:00 P.M.	
11:00 P.M.	
Midnight	
1:00 A.M.	
2:00 A.M.	
3:00 A.M.	
4:00 A.M.	
5:00 A.M.	

Being willing to be honest about your use of time supports you in reevaluating what matters most. Acknowledge yourself each hour you are living by your commitments.

Day 17

Excuses

We all have excuses. Excuses about why we haven't fallen in love lately to why we are overweight to excuses about our job and why we don't feel fulfilled. Excuses tie us up, keep us down, and convince us they are necessary to make us safe. In order to hold this mind-set in place, we must work diligently, usually unconsciously, to create more excuses that validate the ones that already exist. Excuses become the evidence we need to prove we are right in spite of being wrong.

It is natural to build evidence to prove the reality of your excuses. We all do it. If you like Calvin and you want Calvin to like you back, you will begin to notice any little thing that will prove that he does. If he smiles at you one second longer than normal or laughs just a little louder at your jokes, in your mind he is secretly, telepathically, telling you he likes you. If you like Calvin but don't think you deserve him, you will start to think he isn't interested. And you have evidence to prove it: He turned away when you were looking at him, he didn't smile when you passed him in the hall, he didn't call you back right away. Building evidence either sets you free or keeps you stuck.

When you are building evidence you are putting faith in your excuses. You can do such a good job proving excuses exist that they become very real to you and very hard to break. For instance, let's say you don't think you have enough time. What do you focus on? Proving to yourself that you don't have enough time. You notice when you can't get something done due to time constraints, when you are late, etc.

Excuses seem so real that they can be difficult to give up. Many people have created an entire life based on their excuses. For many years I hid my big excuse. June 15, 1975. It was a Sunday and in my little town Sundays meant church services and family gatherings. The same was true in my family. We loved nothing better than to go out for Sunday brunch. Today was Father's Day.

It was an extra special Sunday because my mother and father had recently separated. They had already been divorced once and had re-married a year later, so when they separated again it didn't faze me or my sisters. I had two. Cindy was four years older. At eighteen she was a new mother. Her son Jason had been born just a few months before. My parents were thrilled to have their first grandson. My father had always wanted a boy and now he had one.

My little sister, Linda, was thirteen. We were only a year and a half apart in age but two grades. She had the unpleasant experience of fol-lowing me in school, and since it was such a small school, she would invariably get the same teachers I had. But I was teacher's pet and she loathed it. They would greet Linda with the dreaded words: "Oh, you must be Rhonda's sister." She hated me for years.

This Sunday we decided to get along for the sake of my mother. The separation was stressful for her. She had broken out in hives days before and I had just found Prozac in the cupboard. No one took antidepressants in my little town. It was unheard of. It made me re-alize how much the divorce was taking out of her.

As my mother was getting ready in her blond-furniture bedroom, I was trying to gather my sisters together. I was always on time when we were going to have my favorite Sunday brunch at the Douglas House Hotel. It was a rare event now that my parents were parting ways.

My father walked into the house smiling and yelling, "Let's go!" My father was the type of man who, when he was in a crowd, was charming, but when you were alone with him, he could be moody and unpredictable. But at fourteen I was more interested in being cool than getting along with my dad. Linda was Daddy's girl. I had never even been considered for the role.

I remember one time months before my father moved out, I was walking up the basement steps and he was walking down. He didn't like what I had on or the smirk I perpetually wore. When a smart com-ment escaped my lips, he lunged at me. But I was too fast. By the time he raised his hand, I was up the stairs and running toward my room.

If I could just get to my room and shut the door, maybe he would cool down. Maybe he would run into Linda. Maybe the phone would ring. I remember just thinking to myself, Get to my room. And I did. But so did he. Seconds later he was on top of me with his hands around my throat squeezing hard. I was kicking him trying to get him off me. It was no use. Even though he was only five foot nine, he was strong. And soon I was drifting in and out of consciousness, waiting to die. At that moment I heard Linda's voice loud and clear.

"Daddy, Daddy, quit killing Rhonda. Daddy, stop. Daddy. Don't kill Rhonda." She repeated it over and over again. His hands relaxed and I rolled over, choking and spitting up while trying to breathe again. I don't remember my sister coming over to check on me. I don't remember my father ever saying he was sorry. I don't remember my mother asking me about it. It became another little dirty secret our family kept to itself.

But today was going to be different. We were going out to celebrate my dad. He would be in a good mood. We even bought presents. My mind wandered to the possibility of my mom and dad having fun together. I wanted to keep that thought in my mind. Maybe even make it come true. I decided to play the perfect daughter as my dad went to get his coat while I got everyone into the car.

My sisters were fighting it out in the bathroom when my mother and I decided to put the pressure on by going and sitting in the car. This was always the last resort. Can you imagine sitting in the car to get people to cooperate? But that is what happened in my family. Car sitting was the norm. It was my turn to do it.

Letting out one more "Hurry," I walked outside while my mother was walking toward her car to open the doors. My father was busy in the trunk of his car trying to find his coat. That's when I saw it. I didn't believe it at first. It was so surreal. But there it was: a rifle. And he was pointing it at my mom. She had noticed it about the same time I had but it was too late, she was trapped. My father had conveniently parked his car very close to my mother's so when she opened the driver's door, there was no way to slip by. She was now stuck between her car door and the rifle.

He began yelling at my mother, "You made me do this. This is your fault." She was just shaking her head and saying over and over, "Don't you do this, Ron. Don't you do this." She didn't beg. She didn't plead. But she tried in vain to cover her body with her arms while he waved his gun just a few feet away. The bullet hit her. She didn't fall but lurched forward grasping her stomach.

Frozen on the back porch, I started screaming, "Daddy, I will take care of you. I will live with you." Just days before my father had asked my mother if I would live with him. I was shocked by his request. Everyone knew Linda was his favorite. I was more of an afterthought and someone he tried to ignore. But now he was asking for me. In that moment I thought he might actually love me. Maybe if I sacrificed myself and lived with him, my mother would be saved. I repeated my offer until the gun was pointed at me. I thought it was my turn to die.

With one glance he shut me up and got back to business. He cocked his rifle a second time and pointed it squarely at my mother, who was completely defenseless. The second bullet went right through her and landed in the car horn. For the next twenty minutes the car horn blared until the paramedics could dismantle it. By the time they showed up, my mother was dead. But not before my father did one final act.

When my mother fell into the car and the horn started blasting, my father began to run toward me. As I watched him fall to his knees, I noticed he was cocking his rifle a third time. Wondering if it was my turn, I started to scream but instead he aimed it at his head, and within seconds, he fired. My father had decided to die at my feet. His blood splattered against my brand-new white cotton dress my mother had just made for me. It was over. I was still standing. I didn't want to be. As my sisters began to realize what was happening, they ran over to the American Legion across the street to get help. It was too late. My sisters and I were now orphans.

From that moment on their death became my biggest excuse. Not being loved by your father is bad enough, but watching him take himself and your mother away added insult to injury. My father slapped my face when he didn't take me with him that day and then again, when my words meant nothing. I wasn't worth killing and I wasn't worth living for. I had always had a sneaking suspicion that was true but now it had become a fact, an excuse I could point to for the rest of my life.

That excuse haunted me for years, so when I went away to college I prayed it would be a fresh start. No one would have to know my

history. Being the daughter of a murderer was not something I
wanted to become common knowledge. I just wanted to be known for
me and me alone, not for a deed my father had done years ago. But
college proved too painful because of my parents. My excuses gave
me the right to assume, expect, and defend anything against anyone.
Any relationship I tried to form ended up as a failure. My excuses felt
real and insurmountable, but all excuses can.

Your true self would never accept excuses. It doesn't believe, see,
or even contemplate that excuses are real. Ask yourself: If you were
fearless, would you still have your same excuses? I doubt it. Excuses
only exist because we choose to keep them alive by continuing to validate their existence.

In order to move past my excuses I had to face them. I had to
admit they existed. It wasn't easy. Sometimes I felt I deserved to be
miserable. I mean, how can you be happy if your parents are dead?
I thought being a good daughter meant a life filled with suffering but
years later, I wanted to live. But I had to give up my excuses to do it.

The following questions are a good test to find your excuses:

If only _____ hadn't happened, my life would be better.
If only I could _____, my life would be better.
You don't understand, I can't because _____.

Intellectually, you may realize your excuses are no longer valid,
yet you haven't stopped using them. Are they still running your life?
Admitting it now will support you in shifting your perspective.

George came to see me because on one hand he was happy with
his job, but on the other he was frustrated about his personal life.
After his bankruptcy at the age of thirty he had started working as a
health consultant. It changed his life. But in regard to his relationships he was still stuck in the past. And his kids didn't help. In his
mind, they saw him as a piggy bank instead of as a dad. With women,
he would end up accusing them of cheating because of his first wife's
indiscretion. George would become jealous for no reason at all. It was
wearing down his relationships.

George had excuses: the way his first wife had left him; going
bankrupt when he was thirty; and having children. His excuses kept
him victimized. He used his fear of being hurt again as his excuse to

be overprotective in relationships. His relationship with his children was corrupted by his fear of being used. George wanted never to feel used again, so any time they asked him for anything, he blew their supposed greed all out of proportion. And his bankruptcy gave him endless excuses, including refusing to get married to his current girl-friend or investing in his business to reach the next level of success.

What are your top three excuses? What are the reasons you say, "No, I can't" or "I shouldn't," or "If only things were different"? Identifying the explanations you say to yourself will help you separate your true self from your fearful self. Your true self would never make excuses. It doesn't even see excuses. Your true self always says, Yes! Yes to more success. Yes to more growth. Yes to risk after risk after risk.

List your top three excuses:

1.
2.
3.

Now you have your top excuses. If you want to start shattering their reality, answer the following question using each excuse.

If my excuse about _____ were no longer true, how would my life change?

1.
2.
3.

This exercise was difficult for George. It is hard for most people to come to grips with how much their excuses have been running their lives. He had invested too much of his energy and made so many decisions based on their reality. But each excuse we create gives us a benefit in some way or another. They make us feel better about ourselves for a while but usually at the expense of something else.

I asked him to answer the following question. You do the same.

How do I benefit from having _____ excuse?
Or in other words,
What do you gain from having _____ excuse?

Be honest. Is there some way that keeping your excuses actually makes you appear to be a better person, a more saintly person, a harder working person? For George his divorce only gave him ammunition about how caring he was and how uncaring she was. His inability to get over his bankruptcy kept proving to others how responsible he was now. His children proved to be an area where he could acknowledge himself. So the tougher the time his kids had, the more amazing he became as a father. He gained a warped sense of self-confidence. I say "warped" because true confidence cannot be built on other people's failings.

If you are having trouble with the benefit/gain question, you might want to think of it this way: there is a positive to every problem. Because of George's divorce excuse he could say he is more loving. How wonderful. Do you see why George might benefit from keeping his excuse about his divorce alive? It continually reinforces, once again, his "warped" self-confidence because it makes him feel better about himself at the expense of another. When we compare ourselves to someone else, we will not gain true self-confidence. True confidence is the result of our own internal battles.

Go ahead. Think of it this way.

Because of _____ excuse, I can say I am _____
_____.

Our excuses stay alive past their usefulness when we grow attached to the reason they exist. We become comfortable and familiar with our excuses; they become conversation starters and instantaneous intimacy builders. We find a peculiar kind of safety in our excuses that gives us permission to perpetuate our fears.

George had to quit using his divorce as his excuse for not getting married. He had to own up to whether he wanted to do it or not. Maybe he wasn't ready, but his girlfriend deserved to know the truth. I had to realize that my parents' deaths could be used for growth rather than keeping me a victim. It was the hardest thing I ever did: letting go of my excuse. From that moment on, I would have to be responsible for my actions, thoughts, and feelings. When it would get difficult, it would seem easier to stay small. But I knew that wasn't true. It just felt true when I was scared.

Leaving excuses behind is risky. When we quit leaning on our supposed faults, we must begin to lean on our talents, abilities, and willingness. We give up surviving and start to thrive. We are able to change our destiny.

Today, No More Excuses

Excuses keep you small. They give you permission to blame others for your life. Excuses take your power away and keep you victimized. If you have an excuse, you cannot be true to yourself.

If you had no more excuses, what risks would you take?

If you had no more excuses, how would you be more true to yourself?

What do you fear most at the thought of giving up your excuses?

If I had a magic wand and could aid you in giving up one excuse, which one would it be?

I dare you to eliminate any conversation regarding your top three excuses for the next twenty-four hours. If you only connect to others using your excuses, you will never feel loved for yourself. Learning to give up your excuses will force you to create conversations that speak of possibilities, hope, and love. Be open today.

Intuition

I can't tell you how many times I have been asked, "How can you tell the difference between intuition and the voice of fear?" It seems everyone wants to know the secret.

I find it ironic that the most natural thing in the world is so difficult for so many people. You were born with your intuition. It was loud and clear when you were young, but with every hurt, every disappointment, you have learned to cover it up and shut it down because your intuition can take you into scary territories. With no tools to support you and little self-confidence, trusting yourself was not an option. You have discovered it's safer not to listen to your intuition and instead hear your worries and concerns. Those you know how to handle. They are familiar. You have forgotten that intuition will tell you the difference between what you should do and what you are meant to do. Let me share a story.

"Do you have a brother?"

It was an odd question to ask a man I had known for less than an hour, but it seemed so right. I knew I had to ask or I would bust. His name was Harold and he was seated next to me on a short flight from Denver to Chicago.

Usually I am the last person to start a conversation on a plane, but the week before I had fallen off my bicycle, hurting my arm, and was now having trouble lifting my carry-on luggage into the overhead compartment. I had to ask for help. I asked Harold.

And now I was asking Harold if he had a brother. He did. And he was single.

Richard was thirty-eight years old, four years younger than me, but Harold assured me it didn't matter. With hope in my heart I began the drill.

Does he have male friends? Does he get along with his ex? Can he handle a woman who is on fire with life?

Yes. Yes. Yes.

Richard, a successful real estate broker, was adventurous, a devoted father, and, his brother assured me, the nicest guy on the planet. I could deal with a nice guy, I reasoned.

As we landed, I reminded Harold that I was serious about wanting to meet his brother.

Twenty-four hours later I was on the phone with Richard. Forty-eight hours later we went on our first date. Seventy-two hours later we were crazy about each other.

Fate? Maybe.

Is he The One? Who knows?

Was I being led by my intuition? Absolutely.

Everyone wanted to know how I got up the courage to ask Harold if he had a brother. It was simple. I listened to my intuition. It nudged me into action by giving me unsolicited advice. It does that all the time. It tells me where to go and what to do. I hardly make a move without consulting it.

My intuition is not based on my logic or even my heart. When I ask my intuition for an answer, I am getting input from a source unseen that is bigger than my perceptions. You can call your intuition the voice of God or Allah or Universal Energy. It doesn't matter what it's called, it works the same regardless. Your intuition is here to guide you to fulfill your potential, to be true to yourself above all else.

Let me break down exactly what happened on that plane. I was attempting to lift my luggage into the overhead rack when I realized there was no way I was going to do it with my sore arm. There were at least ten people around me that I could have asked, but I chose Harold. How did I choose Harold? My eyes looked around and when I saw him I knew. It was like I heard a silent yes. I didn't have any idea why Harold was the one to pick, but I have learned never to ask questions when my intuition is helping me make any kind of decision. I just know it is the best thing to do, so I do it.

At this point I didn't even know Harold was going to be sitting next to me, so imagine my surprise when, after he took care of my luggage, he proceeded to sit down smack dab in the next seat. Harold and I were as close as you can get on a plane. I started chatting, wondering what my intuition had in store for me.

We talked about our respective trips. He talked about his wife and kids. Harold was such a family man that it made me yearn for that kind of relationship. That's when I asked about his brother. I was in the moment, fully present to the conversation. Not planning what I was about to say. Your intuition can rarely be heard over your agenda when you aren't willing to be open and flexible.

Do you ever have that urge to talk to a friend? Do you ever want to make a decision that is against all logic but you feel a sense of calm about it? That is what intuition gives you, a sense of calm. Your intuition never rushes you or makes you feel stupid or calls you names. It just is.

That is one of the ways I know it is my intuition, there is no "should" attached to it. No guilt. No "I'd better" or else. No "have to" or something bad will happen. There is only a quiet, silent nudge that brings with it a calm confidence. Now, this is the tricky part. After you get your intuitive hit and begin to take the steps to make it happen, you could get scared, because now you are dealing with the nuts and bolts of reality. Your fear is going to pop up just like we discovered on the Stretch, Risk, or Die Day. That is where most people get sidetracked. They think when their intuition is at work, they will never become afraid, so they begin to doubt themselves. Wrong. Do Not Doubt!

You can't follow your destiny if you can't hear your calling. Your intuition will never leave you high and dry. All you have to do is listen. Most of my life I didn't hear my intuition. I didn't know if I was supposed to go left or right, east or west. My feelings dictated my actions, with miserable results.

I would wonder, Why me, why am I alone? I had no real friends and no real family. I was strictly on my own. As I went through my day I would ignore the flirtations, the random connections, the gifts of potential friendship. There was always a reason they weren't quite right for me. Not my type, I would say. Too old. Too young. Too something. There was always a reason to block my intuition. It never felt secure enough. There was never a guarantee. It was too risky.

When I met Richard, he was a good guy. My intuition told me to go for it. We were intellectually matched and had physical chemistry, but in the end he did not have the commitment I desire. See, I want to get married again. He does not. With a divorce under his belt and two small children, Richard didn't want the responsibilities true love required. After dating several months, we broke up. Not because we didn't care, but because he was convinced he wasn't ready. During this relationship my intuition gave me a gift; it taught me the value of fun. Richard was fun and I hadn't had so much fun in a long time.

My past relationships had their share of fun, but I had never had a relationship that was solely fun. Richard and I didn't have long talks about life and death. We didn't sit home and contemplate our careers. We went out. We laughed. He cooked. It showed me that I am ready for more fun in my life and it won't ruin my career. I can have both. Once again my intuition guided me to the next lesson necessary for me to be more true to myself, be more free.

Let me share another story.

By the time I officially started the Fearless Living Institute, I had created, developed, and been coaching and consulting Fearless Living solo for over six years. I was running on passion. It was an exciting time, yet I knew I had to get help if I was going to provide the type of services I wanted to offer. I casually started looking for a partner, and soon three different organizations wanted to expand my vision into the marketplace.

I was drawn to one organization in particular, but it wasn't logically the best choice. It was over a thousand miles away from my home in Los Angeles, the president and I didn't see eye to eye, and I wasn't convinced they understood my vision. Everything and everyone told me not to go forward with the deal. Now, this is the crazy part. My intuition kept nudging me to choose them. Whenever I would sit down to contemplate my decision or actively grab a piece of paper and write down the pros and cons, no matter what answer I thought I "should" have, I kept hearing, Choose Colorado.

I can't say my intuition is an actual voice, but I do hear words almost as if they are coming from the center of my being. It is silent, knowing, and calm. I think the best way to describe it is by saying that when I hear my intuition I feel an undeniable YES. Empowered, enlightened, and inspired are the attributes I experience, and I just "know." I cannot deny the answer I have been given.

Now, this is the kicker. Your intuition never tells you why you are doing what you are doing. It never tells you the results you will achieve. It only tells you what to do next, and I was, and am, convinced that the decisions I make based on my intuition are the best ones for me at the time. Intuition relies on faith. Faith that you will do what is necessary, no questions asked.

I had a sense of calm about the decision. So I chose Colorado.

The partnership lasted less than a year. From the outside looking in it appeared to be a bad business deal. I lost thousands of dollars and all the hard work that had gone into the Institute seemed to be wasted. But I didn't focus on the results, I focused on the process, the reason why my intuition had brought me here in the first place. There is a gift within every intuitive hit, and it was my job to find what that gift was.

What was the reason my intuition nudged me to move my home from California to Colorado and partner with another company? I learned many things from the experience. I learned how to delegate and found out that I liked working with a team. Even though we had our differences, I enjoyed the collaboration. I was able to live in London, halfway around the world, and become the first coach to change lives on television. I realized that I knew more about business than I gave myself credit for. In the past I had always apologized for my lack of formal training in facilitating groups but when I gave a workshop for over twenty professional facilitators, they gave me a standing ovation. I never doubted myself again. I learned that you have to be willing to forgive not just in your personal relationships but your business ones as well. I learned that even when people have the best of intentions it doesn't mean things are going to turn out like you planned. I found out that I am a woman who thinks long-term rather than short-term. I became more self-confident knowing that no business can define me. I affirmed that I must love what I am doing or no matter how well things are going, I am not happy. And lastly, I learned that the gifts I receive when I follow my intuition serve me better than I can humanly imagine.

You might be saying to yourself I could have had these realizations and experiences with anyone I partnered with and had less stress. Maybe. But I doubt it.

Remember, I was warned. Everyone told me not to do it except my intuition. I trusted it completely. How did I know it was my intuition and not some sadistic part of myself? Well, that is easy. I knew. I didn't get anxious or worried or confused over my decision. I was clear, focused, and content. There was no "have to" or "must," just a sense of everything working in divine order. No pushing, no shoving, no sacrificing. Without a doubt it was as if there were no other options but this one.

Intuition is unattached to the results. I feel empowered when I get an intuitive hit. There is never any rush or confusion. My intuition never seduces me with success. It never tells me, "Do this and you will have it all." Never. It only tells me the next step I must take. My intuition has never steered me wrong. But be warned: Following your intuition doesn't mean you will feel good all the time or that success is guaranteed. At least, not the kind of success most people talk about.

The voice of fear is run by doubt, suspicion, desperation. There is never enough when I make decisions out of fear. Other feelings I could experience are shame, guilt, and blame. It is almost like I "have to" or else. Dreaded consequences fuel the decisions based in fear. If you have ever said, "I'd better," or "I should," you have experienced the voice of fear. If you have ever beaten yourself up over a decision, fear was keeping you confused and frustrated.

Basically, when intuition hits there is a calm, a sense of peace and empowerment, a feeling that there is enough time, that nothing has to happen now. No comparing or competing. On the other hand, fear thrives on either/or. It wants only one winner and decisions must be made now. It feels like you will lose something if you choose another answer, or something bad will happen.

If you can't hear your intuition loud and clear, sit in silence for a few minutes each day. The voice of fear will frantically show up, pointing out all the reasons you have to quit making time for this silly sitting. Ignore it. Keep sitting. You can focus on something if you like, such as a painting or a flower. It will help you stay on task. This is a form of meditation.

As you sit regularly in silence, your intuition will become stronger because it will be heard. Keep listening. If sitting is out of the question, you can do a walking meditation. The purpose of either assists

you in listening to the voices within. It will help you distinguish between the voice of fear that demands attention and your intuitive
voice that calmly waits to be heard.

There are meditation classes throughout the world teaching different types of meditation. Find one that suits you and sign up. Many
can be found in churches and yoga centers for a minimal fee. Learning how to calm your mind and listen within will change your life and
will force you to be true to yourself. Your intuition will accept nothing less.

I have learned to trust my intuition implicitly. When I follow my
intuition, I am clear. Another benefit I have experienced is the fore-
sight to act upon the unexpected opportunities that cross my path.
For example, when I started my business, I wanted to coach only pri-
vate one-on-one clients. It was what I had trained to do. But then the
unthinkable happened: One of my clients asked me to give her employees a seminar based on my philosophy. I immediately said no. I
wasn't trained for that. I don't have the skills, I reasoned. I don't want
to make a fool of myself. And there it was. My wake-up call. The word
fool. The minute I said that word, a word that disempowers me, I
knew I was afraid. When I am afraid, I have a hard time listening to
my intuition. Intuition is about taking risks, fear is about safety. I had
to be willing to feel like a fool if I was going to hear my intuition. To
trust, to have faith in that voice, you must be willing to experience
anything, even feeling like a fool. I taught the seminar.

Let's look at the decisions you are faced with today. It could include decisions like where you are going to eat, how you are going to
raise your sales quota, or how to deal with a disgruntled employee (or
mate).

Tell me a decision you must make today: _____

Please list your top three answers for this decision:

1.
2.
3.

What feelings come up when you contemplate that answer as the
one?

1.
2.
3.

Remember, your intuition will support you in growth and transformation. It will push you to become more. Fear bases its decisions on holding its ground. It doesn't want to lose. It is afraid to be vulnerable. It will compare and contrast every tidbit before it will decide. And it will decide based on the least chance of losing. Fear holds on. Intuition breaks loose.

Can you tell what answer is best for you?

When my feelings align with my decisions, I am one within myself. And the world seems more connected, more things are possible, more growth is happening. When that occurs, I think of God. Does your relationship with your intuition mirror your relationship with God or your higher power or Allah? Who else could be behind that still small voice of intuition? I think intuition is a handy word for the voice of God. How else would I know what I know what I know? I practice having faith as I give up my way and follow God's way, using the voice of intuition as the pathway.

If being right is important to you, you will have difficulty hearing your intuition. If you aren't willing to feel stupid, rejected, or silly, you won't be able to listen effectively. When you are willing to live in the unknown, intuition can be heard. When you are willing to be wrong about everything, intuition gets clear. When you are judging less and loving more, intuition feels like it is coming directly from within you.

One of the main drawbacks that kept intuition from working in my life was my belief that it could not be my intuition. It was scary to think that I would know what to do in the midst of the unknown. It was easier to blame someone else than to claim I had the answer within through my intuition. It was a lesson in believing the still, silent voice rather than my loud, nervous voice of fear.

And that is the main difference: the tone of the voice. I can spot a decision made out of fear within minutes. The tone of fear is desperate. It harbors judgment, shame, and projects feelings of selfishness and control. It makes you feel stupid and worthless. Like someone who emotionally abuses you, it uses your desires against you to prove that you are not good enough. The voice of my intuition never makes me feel stupid for being me. I don't feel like I am going to be punished if I don't act immediately. I know it sounds corny, but I feel loved.

Listening objectively to the voices within will support you in separating the voice of fear from your intuition more quickly. Detach yourself from what the voice is saying and instead focus on the tone, and you will tell the difference. Fear will be demanding, while intuition will support. Fear will tell you to get it now, while intuition will tell you to go at your own pace.

Learning to listen to your intuition will make a profound impact on your life. My relationship with God unfolded most miraculously when I started to listen. Imagine that God has an assignment for each one of us and all we have to do is ask. The problem is if we ask, we must be able to hear the answer. Can you hear the voice of God directing you to your next step? If so, be prepared for miracles.

Today, Listen to Your Intuition

Being able to hear the difference between the voice of fear and your intuition is critical if you want to be true to yourself. It is easy to be fearless when intuition is your guiding force. Let's practice.

Tell me the difference between the voice of fear and your intuition.

When was the last time you heard your intuition?

What decisions in your life have you made intuitively?

If you don't hear your intuition regularly, how do you make decisions?

Admitting that intuition may be something you crave rather than regularly experience is a moment of truth. It is vital to separate results from the journey. Together we are working on understanding how you process information related to your intuition.

For the next twenty-four hours I want you to list all the times you listen to your intuition. It may be once or twice or not at all. The number doesn't matter. It is the commitment to observe that will eventually make the difference. Let go of your desire for results and your intuition will be heard loud and clear.

My intuitive moments in twenty-four hours:

Day 19

Forgiveness

Monica didn't particularly like the way her boss treated her. She thought he was rude and spoke to her in a loud voice, demanding things and generally being, in her mind, mean. She wanted to quit her job.

"Tell me how your boss is mean to you," I asked.

"Well, he is loud, and brash and generally just pushes me around," she exclaimed. As she shared her disdain for the man, her voice got shrill and she flung her arms wildly around. She was clearly upset.

"Obviously, his behavior affects you greatly. He seems to have a lot of power over you."

"What? Power over me? Well, I guess he does. Anyone that mean would want to have all the power. I'm just too nice, I guess."

"Too nice?" I questioned her logic.

When fear is running a part of your life, it is easy to point the finger at the seeming source of the problem rather than look inside for the fear that is giving you permission to sit on the sidelines.

"Have you tried to talk to him? Have you forgiven yourself for allowing someone to treat you that way?"

"Forgive myself? Why should I forgive myself? He is the one who is mean."

"And you? Are you mean to yourself when you don't stand up for yourself? Are you mean to yourself when you refuse to put up a boundary that will help you feel respected and appreciated? Have you forgiven yourself for being 'too nice' at the expense of your self-esteem?" I was on a roll.

Monica quietly murmured, "I never thought about it like that before."

"Most people don't. Yet, each time we blame someone else for our mood or blame him or her for our desire to run away, we are giving away our power. We are the ones who have let ourselves down by refusing to learn new skills in order to handle the situation differently, or we put ourselves last by ignoring the need for a boundary. We constantly undermine our own self-confidence and blame someone else for doing it, when in truth we are doing it to ourselves."

"Rhonda, are you saying I could change this situation?"

"Sure, you could and you can. It could include speaking to your boss differently or learning to stay centered and positive regardless of his treatment or walking away from the job because it truly does not serve you. All of those are options and there are so many more." And then I asked the hard question: "Has this happened before?"

Monica's sense of injustice was no longer pointing to her boss now, it was pointing at her.

"Yes. It has. I just figured I attracted rude bosses. I didn't think I had anything to do with it."

"Monica, I am not saying you are causing their behavior, but I am saying you can change the way you react toward him. And who knows what could happen. Minimally, you will learn a new way to speak, act, and think when someone seems to be rude to you."

Learning to forgive yourself for the ways you put yourself last will help you put the past behind you. If you can't forgive yourself, the likelihood of you achieving clarity is reduced. Forgiveness provides clarity and clarity encourages insights and that supports a change in behavior. When you forgive yourself or another, it does not mean you agree with their behavior, but rather it is about letting go of your need to be right so you can move forward.

Learning to forgive another yet not forgetting their behavior will support you in learning what boundaries to erect. Boundaries must be honored in order for you to feel safe. For instance, one of Monica's boundaries could be that no one can yell at her. It shuts her down, she can't think, and she is out of commission. Yelling doesn't support the process of change. Therefore, Monica may request a "no yelling zone."

Monica must have the courage to express her boundary and then be willing to enforce it. Enforcing is the tough part. We can complain without end about what we don't want, but unless it becomes a spoken nonnegotiable, something that must happen in order for us to continue the relationship, the boundary will not be taken seriously.

When Monica puts boundaries in place and enforces them daily, she will be teaching herself and the other party what behaviors she will accept in her relationships. Learning to stand for yourself builds your self-esteem.

Monica must not only forgive herself for her less than perfect actions, she must be willing to forgive all those folks who did less than kind things to her. Again, it doesn't mean forgetting and accepting their behavior. It means seeing the intent behind the action. It means understanding if anyone does anything to you that is mean, or rude, it indicates that fear is running their life.

When we are afraid of someone or something, we usually aren't as loving or kind or compassionate as we could be. We need to ask for help. Yet, many times when we are afraid we are unable to admit that we feel vulnerable, because we are in protect mode. When we are trying to protect ourselves, the last thing we want to do is become vulnerable. But it is the very thing we must do.

Monica had to forgive herself for accepting her boss's behavior and she also had to forgive him. I asked Monica to reach out to a coworker or a friend when she felt paralyzed by his behavior. Writing up a list of unacceptable behavior will help determine if boundaries were crossed, because feelings can keep us confused about the situation.

In essence it is never about blaming another person's behavior for your unhappiness. It is always about your own actions. No one can change another person, therefore do not be fooled by empty promises. Actions speak louder than words. Monica not only had to assert her boundaries out loud but she had to act on them.

How do you forgive yourself?* It begins with a willingness to let go of the past. Not give in, but instead surrender. If Monica forgave herself, no longer would her guilty feelings determine her actions. Right

---

*In my first book, *Fearless Living*, I describe in detail how I forgave my parents and myself for their tragic and untimely deaths. If you want to read more about forgiveness, please refer to Chapter Seventeen: Excuses.

now, Monica was not standing up for herself because she was afraid she would lose her job. Whenever you are afraid to lose, you will always be run by fear.

True forgiveness is a moment-by-moment experience. Daily we must take our less than loving moments and be willing to see ourselves as human. In our willingness to forgive we are able to embrace our humanity. The freedom to be true to who you are lies in your willingness to see yourself as human—no better, no less, than any other human on this amazing earth.

In 1776 the Declaration of Independence was signed, claiming "that all Men are created equal, that they are endowed by their Creator with certain unalienable Rights, that among these are Life, Liberty, and the Pursuit of Happiness." When I read that statement I can imagine the level of forgiveness each of the signers must have achieved before he could sign a document that would change the history of the world. You can't write a statement like "all Men are created equal" without a sense of something larger than yourself at play. And that is where forgiveness comes in.

Forgiving yourself or another is an important step in leaving the past behind and stepping into the future. In order to forgive another you must be willing to see that the majority of people rarely do anything purposely to hurt, betray, or disappoint you. They have the best of intentions but their intentions are misguided because of their own fears, lack of skills, and level of awareness. They do not know. Their core needs drive them to behave in ways they are hardly proud of. Your inability to forgive validates their unworthiness, only causing them greater shame, pushing them farther and farther away from their true self. The same thing happens to you. If you are not willing to forgive yourself, on some level you are saying it is a punishment to stay small.

When you are willing to forgive yourself for your mistakes and misgivings, your life is a clean slate. You experience a sense of ease and release that you may not even know at this time is possible. It is hard to imagine a life without guilt or shame, but that is what's possible when forgiveness becomes a daily calling and an experience that is honored.

And so much of the hurt of the world can be alleviated by the simple words "I'm sorry." The first step in forgiveness. Yet, for most people it is the hardest thing to say. To many it implies guilt, an admission that they are wrong. Saying "sorry" goes much deeper than claiming blame for a particular situation. In many ways, "sorry" clears the air between two people more than any other word. What Monica wanted was an acknowledgment from her boss that he did treat her poorly. She wanted to hear, "I'm sorry."

There are many reasons to say you're sorry. The most important is when you have hurt another and want their forgiveness for a wrong you've committed. But there are other times it is appropriate to say, "I'm sorry," without taking the blame. Here are the different ways and reasons to say it.

"I'm sorry" is so valuable to the healing process. When two people disagree, the more fearless you are the more you are willing to go first. It might not mean you intentionally hurt the other, but as I share below, there are many ways to say "I'm sorry" that don't imply guilt but do imply understanding and compassion.

Saying, "I'm sorry you hurt," validates another person's feelings without agreeing that you had a part in their pain. It lets them know you see their pain and have compassion and empathy for their situation. This phrase helps any time you are listening to another talk about a grievous event in their life, whether you were a part of it or not.

When we refuse to validate another's feelings, it is usually because we are fearful of what that would mean to us. Maybe we think that in some way it would label us wrong or unkind or worthless. But validating another never labels us anything. Rather, validating another's pain is a gift we give by supporting them to move beyond their fear.

Saying, "I'm sorry it didn't work out," lets another know you are listening. It also gives them an opportunity to process their feelings. Giving an individual that gift allows them to move through their uncomfortable feelings without other people's opinions interfering with their own.

When we refuse to listen, we must ask ourselves if we can hear our own inner voice over the fear that is running so much of life. Learning the art of listening is a powerful tool toward fearless intimacy and self-empowerment.

Saying, "I'm sorry we don't agree," gives someone the space to love even in the midst of potential turmoil. Understanding that loving another does not mean you will always agree, allows the two of you to share more of who you are without fear of rejection, ridicule, or resentment.

Saying, "I'm sorry if you feel I hurt you," implies the individual blames you for their pain; yet you are not saying you agree, but rather you are sorry they believe you're responsible. It validates their feelings without taking the blame when you don't agree with their evaluation.

When we refuse to stand for our beliefs, we are stating to the world that our values, principles, and ethics can be swayed. And when we refuse to honor another's beliefs, we are saying that we are right and they are wrong. That in some way what we believe is better. Agreeing to disagree honors individual commitments and beliefs. This expands our ability to receive and give love.

Saying, "I'm sorry if I hurt you," puts the responsibility into your hands when you agree that, yes, you did hurt them. It does not mean you purposely hurt them. It means you take responsibility for your part, even though it was unintended.

When we refuse to take responsibility for hurting someone, fear is pushing us farther away from potential intimacy and toward isolation. It is easy to blame the injured party for feeling upset and to push the responsibility back on him or her. And, yes, we are—in the end—responsible for how we feel. Yet, most of us know when we have said something punishing or hurtful or angry to another. Those are the times when we must step up and admit we hurt someone because our own fear was at work. Without that accountability, trust is elusive.

I want to warn you that saying, "I'm sorry," as a regular part of your everyday conversation takes away its power. We have all met people who say they're sorry about everything. That is not what we are discussing. Saying it over and over implies you are so afraid of being rejected that you will take responsibility for just about everything. I urge you to examine your penchant for apologizing through fresh eyes.

During my divorce I went through a period of deep anguish and pain. My soon-to-be ex-husband was an easy target for my frustration. One afternoon as we were going through the mail my fear of being rejected showed up as tears and fits of rage. He was baffled by my behavior and asked, "What do you want from me?" And I answered, "I just want you to say you are sorry."

I am not alone. Many people stay connected to their pain because they are still waiting to hear those words. My father can never verbally tell me he is sorry. Many friends have never said those words when it was all I desired. I am sure I have not said them nearly enough. We don't always hear it from the people we need to hear it from the most. And if we don't, forgiveness is in order. You must forgive the other person for not understanding your needs, for being unwilling to take responsibility for their part or not listening when you needed to be heard. And perhaps you ought to forgive yourself for the blame, shame, and resentment you feel—or maybe forgive yourself for not asking for what you need.

Another way to heal is to get better at saying "sorry" to others as well as to yourself. I have been getting better. Better at acknowledging another's pain without taking the blame for it. Better at acknowledging their hurt when it has nothing to do with me. Better at acknowledging when I did indeed do something that caused pain to another. Better at saying, "I'm sorry," to myself each time I break a promise or let myself down. Better at clearing the air even when I am afraid to do just that.

I have learned saying, "I'm sorry," sets me free from fear. It is the first step in forgiving another or asking for forgiveness.

Today, Forgive

When we are willing to face the areas where we have been less than our best, forgiveness is in order. Saying, "I'm sorry," takes courage. Today is the day to set yourself free through forgiveness.

Who do you blame for any of your problems or difficulties?

What part of your life is on hold because you have refused to forgive?

If you could hear, "I'm sorry," from anyone, who would it be? Have you forgiven them?

Who have you refused to say, "I'm sorry," to?

Learning to forgive can be challenging, but it is the true path to freedom. For the next twenty-four hours I want you to be in a state of forgiveness. For anyone whom you have wronged, hurt, or punished, admit it and say, "I'm sorry." Pay attention to the folks who you want to punish or hurt; forgiveness is in order—forgiving them for something they may have done and yourself for keeping a record of the hurt.

Learning to forgive is an essential skill to being true to yourself. Without forgiveness your past will forever interfere with your future. If you want to change your life, be willing to forgive and face your unforgiving ways. There is no need to beat yourself up. On the contrary, every time you recognize a place of unforgiveness, acknowledge yourself. You are being fearless!

Day 20

Momentum

You have been going strong for twenty days. You have learned new skills and faced some fears. You have had realizations and insights that will impact the rest of your life. I am sure there have been days when you wanted to quit. But you persevered.

Learning so much in a short period of time is a stellar accomplishment. Most people don't want to take such a stringent self-inventory of themselves. The last twenty days you have been building the momentum that will propel the permanent changes you seek. You have ten more days to absorb all you can about fulfilling your potential. Together, let's continue to turn your hard work into a new you.

Please take a moment and fill in the blanks:

My desire for balance in my life makes me feel _____.

If I stay true to my _____, I will automatically have more balance in my life.

The lie I most frequently tell is _____.

When I lie, I do it because _____.

Excuses excuse me from facing my _____.

I have used _____ as an excuse for as long as I can remember.

My biggest regret is _____.

If I had been aware of my core need _____, my life would be different because _____.

If you want to get what you want you must be willing to go _____.

I want _____ to help me _____.
The words I most frequently use that keep me stuck are
_____.
I am practicing loving myself by giving up the word or phrase
_____.
I know it is my intuition when _____.
The biggest difference between the voice of fear and my intuition
    is _____.
I must trust _____ in order to trust others.
In order to build trust, I must _____.
My unwillingness to forgive _____ is holding me back.
In order to change my life I must forgive myself for _____
_____.

The fill-in-the-blanks lets you know how much you have absorbed and retained from the previous ten days. Being able to see yourself differently is a key factor in learning how to be true to yourself. In the past I would tell myself over and over "I can't" change because my results were not immediate. The last twenty days are here to prove that you can change and change a lot if you stay focused and committed.

Being committed is the foundation of momentum. And being courageous and willing enough to change your commitments as you grow is vital to healthy self-esteem. For the past twenty days you have been discovering more of who you are and how you can manifest greater potential. Keeping it going will take commitment.

List your top three commitments as of Day Twenty. Do not mimic your answers in the previous chapters if they no longer serve you. This is the time to reevaluate your growth. Do not be afraid to change.

My top three commitments are:

1.
2.
3.

At Day Twenty you have just completed almost three weeks of grueling self-development work. Let's integrate.

My top three insights are:

1.
2.
3.

Being willing to claim the insights you have experienced will help them shift into new ways of being. Insights are one thing, but unless you ground them in reality, they will not affect your life permanently. They will help you gain momentum for learning more of life's lessons in a short period of time.

Lessons are things you have learned and then applied to your life. I have learned to say I love you but I will not receive a gift from those words unless I use them in my relationships. The application of the things you have gained turn them into lessons that you can use the rest of your life.

The biggest lesson I learned so far is _____.
It has changed my life because _____.

One lesson I have learned is that giving up lies is not easy. I lied about my parents' deaths for over twenty years. I really believed their deaths were insignificant to the world, so I made them insignificant when I talked to anyone else. How wrong I was. But the lies kept perpetuating my false beliefs. What lies have you given up since staying true to yourself has become a top priority?

Lies are told for a variety of reasons but usually, we tell ourselves, for the benefit of somebody else. Yet, as we have learned, our lies do not only benefit another—we gain something as well. What have been the rewards of lying in the past? When there are benefits to be realized, lies can be seductive. What have you learned about yourself that will support you in giving up lying for good?

One thing I know is when I lie, it proves I have low self-esteem. It takes away my courage to change. When I lie, my momentum decreases because I have put another above myself. But I am no longer interested in living my life for another while sacrificing myself. My needs are just as valuable as anyone else's. That was a hard lesson for me to learn. Probably one of the hardest. Sacrifice has been part of my family's generational experience. If I sacrificed for another, it meant

I was a good person, or so I was taught. Sacrifices steal momentum. Change cannot happen.

Momentum allows you to leapfrog experiences and turn your ability to stretch into risk. You are able to change more rapidly because you are getting used to being comfortable being uncomfortable. In a good way. It is the old adage: being comfortable in your own skin. I think when we accept ourselves for who we are, we are more likely to alter when insights happen. On the other hand, trying to fight for our limitations by using excuses to validate why we are where we are stops us short of becoming true to ourselves.

List three risks you have taken in the past twenty days that, prior to reading this book, would have been unthinkable.

1.
2.
3.

Growth supports growth. Congratulations for taking the steps in the past twenty days to risk what is possible.

Now it is time to take the risk of asking for what you want. In the past twenty days, where have you taken a risk and asked for something you would have previously avoided? List your top three requests.

1.
2.
3.

Asking for what you want and being willing to go first are two keys to end any victim mentality and become a leader. Do you want to be the leader in your life? What requests would you make? Give me your top three.

1.
2.
3.

The ability to make requests informs the world of your needs and gives others the power to fulfill them in a way that empowers you. In the past twenty days you may have realized requests you have that you didn't even know you had. What are they? List one example of a request you have that has remained unfulfilled because of your judgments. Maybe the request seems stupid or selfish to you. No request is.

Tell me yours now:

Part of letting go of your judgments includes letting go of language that has been holding you back. Language is powerful. It truly reflects what we believe. If you say, "I can't," somewhere within you you believe you can't. When you eliminate words that stop you from shining, your star will rise faster and brighter.

Another way to shine brighter is by giving yourself credit for the changes you have been making. When you do so, once again your momentum increases. You can count on yourself more. You believe your intuition and no longer stay stuck in confusion. You see that you have been capable of so much change in just the past twenty days that you wonder, Now what?

"Now what?" is right. Ask yourself: Now that I have been making the necessary changes to be true to myself, what is possible for me now? How could my life change? Go ahead and write down what comes to mind.

Now what is possible for me? Now what could happen to me?

And it is possible. You have been creating momentum over the past twenty days with every stretch, risk, or die you have taken. And with so much growth, possibilities will be coming your way that you could never have expected or even wished for. That's another great bonus of change. Your ability to contemplate your future becomes larger. The unknown is less scary. Things that seemed impossible are possible. This gives you wonderful opportunities to practice listening to your intuition.

When we talked about honing your intuition a couple of days ago, I urged you to start listening. Have you? Have you been honoring that voice within that has the power to guide you through the unknown? When you begin to listen to your intuition, when the voice becomes clear, it is hard to ignore. Your job for the rest of our days together is to become a student of your intuition. Allow it to teach you.

Perhaps you picked up this book because you just knew it was for you. That was your intuition talking. I would like you to list five times you have acted on your intuition in the past twenty days. It will help you see that you are already doing better than you think.

I heard my intuition and acted on it when:

1.
2.
3.
4.
5.

Your intuition is a powerful ally that no one can take away from you. It is more valuable than money or time. It will accurately guide you if you just let it. If you believe in it and court it, it will serve you well.

Part of learning to trust your intuition is learning to trust yourself. You have been doing that over the past twenty days. Trust is so elusive, yet it is the cornerstone of any intimate relationship. Everyone tells me at one time or another when we are working on improving relationships, "I want to trust more." It's like a load-bearing wall. You must have it or the place will collapse. The same is true for you. Without trust many of the tools we have talked about will be of no use. You just won't have the confidence to act.

Can trust be cultivated? Absolutely.

Everyone needs momentum to make dramatic changes. The purpose of the past twenty days of skill building and tool gathering has been to create small changes within you so that so-called large changes can happen with more ease. They will. But you must continue to honor your journey with every step you take. Give yourself kudos for the hard work you have achieved. Please share five of your favorite personal acknowledgments that you have written down over the past twenty days.

1.
2.
3.
4.
5.

Acknowledgments access your courage. Continue to acknowledge yourself throughout our next ten days together. Acknowledgments are crucial to creating permanent change. Temporary change can be gratifying for a moment but it will eventually hurt you more than help when you realize the change has not become permanent. But any change can become grounded by acknowledging the process along the way. It makes the change more real, more concrete.

When you have courage, you can let the things that get in your way go. When you remove the blocks and barriers from your path, you can take charge of your journey. In the past those blocks stopped you from growing and those barriers told you you couldn't make it. That was a lie.

As I shared in Day 19, forgiveness is essential to setting you free to be your true self. In order to build momentum, give yourself credit for the opportunities for forgiveness you have identified. List three situations where forgiveness is in order.

1.
2.
3.

Forgiveness heals. I know for myself the twentieth anniversary of my parents' deaths marked a passage for me. My parents died when I was fourteen and I had now lived two-thirds of my life without them and they were still running my life. When I realized I had to let go, that was the moment I wanted to be true to myself more than I wanted to be loved by them. It was a monumental moment of understanding.

You have achieved much in the last twenty days, but it is just the beginning. The days ahead will test you further on your willingness to put yourself first. Changing your life isn't always easy—that's why we are doing this together.

Each day you complete all the exercises, you recommit to being a better you. I have asked things of you that would take months to address if we were coaching one-on-one together. Yet, with your dedication, what would take months is taking thirty days.

Remember, it took me twenty years to change my life. I have put all that experience and wisdom into these pages. Learn from me and my clients' experiences. Apply the stories to your own life and the last twenty days will catapult you farther than you had ever imagined twenty days ago. The next ten will build up speed so you can take a quantum leap forward.

Whether you joined me because you wanted to change your career, your love life, or your health, it doesn't matter. Change is change is change. And you are learning the tools right now to change your life at will. I am teaching you the skills to master your fears so you can master life. Being true to yourself is the intention as well as the key to internal happiness. Let's keep the momentum going. You have a life to change. . . .

Day 21

Luck, Fate, and Destiny

Terry was a petite twenty-eight-year-old with dark wavy hair and piercing blue eyes. She had shown up for our first coaching session wanting to become famous. With a master's degree in theater from UCLA she thought she had done all the right things to prepare for her craft, but after a few auditions and little work Terry was running out of hope.

"What do you think the problem is?" I asked.

"I have thought about it a lot and I have finally reached the conclusion that acting is all a matter of luck and I haven't been lucky," said Terry.

"That's a handy excuse."

She was not happy with my blunt comment, but it was time to wake up this actor who had been waiting to be discovered.

"Terry, have you felt empowered or disempowered believing luck is the answer?" I asked.

"What does it matter? Luck *is* the answer."

I asked again. "Do you feel empowered or disempowered when you use luck as an excuse for your unemployment?"

"Disempowered. Yes, that's it. I feel disempowered because nothing is in my control. No one wants to take a chance on someone without credits. And trust me, I've tried, but it's just a vicious circle. You need an agent to get auditions but you can't get an agent without acting experience. Everybody knows success comes down to who you know and a good dose of luck. Come on, Rhonda, you know that."

Terry's attempt at persuading me of her plight fell on deaf ears. I knew luck had little to do with it. I had to show Terry that leaving her career to chance was not only hurting her confidence, it was shelving her relationship with her true self. She was looking outside of herself for the solution. And that would never bring her success.

Luck is so seductive. We figure if it graces our doorstep, all our problems will be solved. The lottery will be won. Our beloved will return. The seas will part and the sun will rise upon us. Luck leaves our lives to chance. Chance is great if it falls in our favor, but if not, we can get bitter, resentful, and lead unhappy lives.

I asked Terry to create a list. What things in her life does she have control over and what things doesn't she have control over? Luck and control have an interesting relationship that we will talk about in a minute. You do the same.

Things you have control over:	Things you have no control over:
1.	1.
2.	2.
3.	3.
4.	4.
5.	5.

Under the things she had control over, Terry included taking acting lessons, getting photos taken, pulling her résumé together, maintaining her physical appearance, and showing up to auditions on time.

Things she didn't have control over included whether or not she got hired, what jobs were available for her type, if her résumé and photo impressed anyone, and if she was liked.

I pointed out to Terry that she had control over many things in her acting career. She determined what she would wear to her photo session and who she would hire to snap the shutter. Acting classes were completely under her control. Did she take the best classes she could and attend regularly? When it came to her résumé, she had the ability to make it stand out. Her mailings to casting agents also were under her control. Follow-up phone calls, auditioning for plays, invites to showcases, and so on, were all under Terry's control.

To make sure she understood how much control she really had, I asked her to rate how well she was achieving what she had control over. You can also fill it in for yourself.

	Rating scale
Things you have control over:	**1 (lowest) to 10 (most effort)**
1.	
2.	
3.	
4.	
5.	

Terry couldn't believe the results. She had always thought she had little control over her career, but this exercise proved she did. She could make a difference. Terry rated herself a ten for photos but a three on acting classes and a four on physical appearance. Terry's average score ended up being a five. Basically she invested in her career fifty percent of the time. That's not enough. She had no idea she had been putting so little effort into her acting career. She had been blind because she had blamed her lack of luck for her failed career.

"I thought I was working so hard. But now I see I haven't been working hard on the things that I can control that could make a difference," Terry confessed. Terry worked hard, all right. She worked hard at waiting, complaining, and preparing to be a famous actress but not on her craft. Terry wanted to be discovered. She was waiting for luck to strike.

No one has control over everything. It isn't possible. Yet if you do your best in the areas that you *can* impact, the areas that you *can't* will allow you to learn to trust the process, an important aspect of being true to yourself. I am sure you have heard the saying that luck is when opportunity and hard work meet. So true.

Using luck as your excuse for failure also inhibits your ability to give yourself credit. Because if luck is the reason you have failed, you are going to use that same rationale for your success. "I was just lucky" is a phrase I despise. When you use it your self-esteem will never increase, because in your mind happenstance determines whether lady luck is going to shine on you. Notice I said "shine on." Such a passive role. I want my light to shine *through* me, not *on* me. Once again, we are learning about another way we deny our good.

When I hear someone say, "I'm just not lucky," I cringe. I want to scream, "Are you doing anything to increase your odds?" When Terry took control of her photos and made sure they were the best they could be, she increased her odds. Buying a lottery ticket is a game of chance, but there are ways you can increase your ability to win. One way is to buy a ticket. Another way is to buy a ticket consistently. And still another is buying a ticket with a group of people so their odds become your odds.

If I had my druthers, no one would use the word *luck*. I think luck does more harm than good. Like Terry most people who focus on luck, or give luck credit for their success, do not have healthy self-esteem. They do not have the ability to repeat their "luck" at choice. Without choice there is no self-empowerment.

If you want to rely on luck, good luck! If you want to rely on yourself, on your support team, on the universe, you will have more ability to make a difference than if you waited for luck to happen.

I invite you to eliminate luck from your vocabulary for the next twenty-four hours. It isn't lucky that you met a friend at Starbuck's. It wasn't fate that attracted your new boyfriend. It wasn't that the stars were aligned correctly that supported your weight loss. You did all of it by showing up and being present. Luck didn't make you do that. You did.

If you take control of what you can, the chances of success are multiplied. You will be ready when the opportunity comes your way. You won't be asking for a break. You will get a break because you have done the work to create the break.

Terry is now on Broadway singing her heart out in a successful musical. It didn't happen because of luck. Terry started to take care of business and the business ended up taking care of Terry.

Similar to luck, fate is seductive. The catch-22 is either everything is based on fate or nothing is. When I hear the word *fate,* I think of destiny or providence. For example, it's as if you could be living in Kansas but if you were destined to fall in love with a man from New York, you would. Somehow you would meet.

When Alice met Beck she was convinced it was fate. Describing their first conversation, Alice was clearly moved and affected by their encounter. But it brings up a question. Didn't Alice have to say hello? Didn't she have to open her eyes? She could have walked away or turned her head or barely listened to him during their first conversation. If she'd had a bad day, she could have been disengaged and just waited to go home. But, on the contrary, Alice decided to participate and engage and connect with Beck.

I told Alice that fate doesn't keep folks together. Commitment does. And if she gives fate all the credit for their connection, fate will also be at fault when they aren't getting along.

I have met many people who knew their mate as a friend years before they got together. Does that mean there is no fate quotient? See, that is the problem with fate. There is no ability to include yourself in the equation. It all happens out there and it seems like you had nothing to do with it, no power over it. It just happens. Nothing just happens.

To put this theory to the test I invite you to assume everything is happening to you today because it is fate. Going to the bank? Fate. Going to work? Fate. Meeting your friend for coffee? Fate. I know it sounds silly, but I am trying to prove a point. What constitutes one experience being fated while another is not?

Don't get me wrong, when it comes to love fate sounds so romantic. Alice agreed.

"I couldn't help myself," she said. "It was if I was drawn to him like a magnet."

They had no choice. It had to happen. Nothing could stand in their way. All are phrases associated with fate. But everyone does have a choice. And nothing had to happen—you had to be willing for it to happen. And lots of things could stand in the way. Fear could definitely get in the way. Notice in all the phrases there is a hint of no responsibility. It goes back to the misperceptions people have about passion. Passion is a big responsibility and so is fate.

I like to think of fate as a beautifully wrapped gift. In order to use fate fully I have to unwrap it, open the box, and read the directions. There are many things to do before I can fully appreciate "fate." I asked Alice to use this metaphor to describe her relationship with Beck.

First, she had to recognize that Beck had nothing to do with fate. She had to see him before she could meet him. Then she'd needed to have the courage to start a conversation. All of that took a lot of confidence. Alice had the confidence to take action because she had been working hard to become fearless. If Alice hadn't had the confidence, she would never have recognized Beck and fate wouldn't have happened.

Think of a fateful experience you have had since beginning our journey together. Maybe even buying this book has felt like fate. Now I want you to give yourself credit for the things that prepared you to recognize, and then have the courage to take action about, your fateful experience.

Fateful experience:

Ability to recognize and act on fate because:

During the next twenty-four hours I would like you to act as if everything is fate. It will help put the experience of fate into perspective. When you do feel something is fate, make sure you acknowledge yourself for all the ways you contributed to that moment. That will help you to continue to build your self-esteem while being grateful for the opportunity that presented itself through fate.

Luck, fate, and *destiny* are words that take your ability to be proactive and make a difference out of the mix. With luck you are an innocent bystander; fate happens to you; and destiny is preordained, giving you no power to change it.

If you look at my life, you might say that my career as a life coach is my destiny. Being a life coach definitely accesses my purpose and allows me to express my passion. And because of my history of healing myself after my parents' death, the argument that it is my destiny to heal lives today is more convincing.

I have thought many times about the concept of destiny and my life. The moment where destiny would have been fulfilled was the moment I chose to become a coach. It was a choice. Did the choice activate my destiny or did my destiny force my choice?

Astrology, psychic readings, tarot cards, all say they can predict our future, our destiny. When we rely on outside forces to tell us what to do, we no longer use the skills and tools we have cultivated, including our intuition. We are missing out on opportunities to think, express, and share who we are.

Destiny is described as when passion and purpose collide. It is a combination of skill, experience, and timing all rolled into one. Most people believe that if you are living your destiny, life is easy. On the contrary. That is where the definition of destiny falters.

Every day I must commit to my life's work. Every single day I must be willing to live in the unknown. And I don't think living in the unknown and destiny go together. Destiny feels final. If you have your destiny you are done. You've got your mission. But to me life is never over. And things can change in a blink of an eye.

In truth, I do not want a sense of destiny to keep me trapped in my current perception of myself. And that is what destiny implies. It almost creates an image that can encapsulate our dream in the moment.

When I need encouragement and support, do I lean on destiny? Yes, I do. When I don't think I can make a difference or when I am not sure what I do matters, telling myself this is my destiny helps me stay positive. It is a reminder that what I do is bigger than me.

And that is the positive aspect of destiny, fate, and luck. There is something bigger than us. We don't have control of everything and we can't make a difference just because we want to sometimes. Learning where you can invest and where you need to let go is a skill.

That is where the seduction of destiny, fate, and luck come into play. I would rather eliminate all those words from your vocabulary until being proactive, responsible, and invested become rote. Where nothing will be left to chance and acknowledging yourself and giving yourself credit will be a daily activity.

Too many times we give away our growth by calling it destiny, fate, or luck. Those three would not manifest themselves if we weren't doing the work. Do the work. Do not wait or rely on the fates stepping in or luck saving you or your destiny calling.

Take action. Be proactive. Learn to count on yourself, ask for help, and your future will unfold beyond your wildest dreams. What you hoped would be your destiny will be insignificant in comparison.

Do the work. Get prepared. An opportunity is coming your way. Will you be ready?

Today, No More Luck, Fate, or Destiny

Relying on the fates to intervene does not allow you to learn who you are in difficult situations. A belief that your destiny will be fulfilled can be your ego talking. If you are waiting for luck to make you a winner, you will be waiting forever. It isn't possible. Today is the day you are giving up luck, fate, and destiny. Put them aside and put yourself in the forefront. Answer the following questions for insights into the power these three words have over your life.

Where have you been using luck as an excuse?

How has believing in fate held you back?

What would happen if you quit relying on luck?

How would your life change if you didn't need to fulfill your destiny?

For the next twenty-four hours, eliminate the words *luck, fate,* and *destiny* from your vocabulary. Pay attention to the times when luck, fate, and destiny are seductive. It is time to count on yourself and create your own future rather than allowing something outside of yourself to determine your results.

Day 22

The Gift of Rejection

Rejection is hard to face. No one likes it.
If you have ever:

- become silent when you wanted to speak your truth
- walked away when, in fact, you wanted to stay
- acted tough when you were melting inside
- started a fight because you were afraid to get close
- turned your back because it seemed easier than standing tall
- silently known you were in love yet never shared it with the object of your desire

You have avoided rejection.

Rejection can appear in many ways. It can be a good friend moving on in his or her life, a spouse who no longer seems interested, a job that doesn't seem to appreciate you, or another common one: you rejecting yourself.

Many of us work so hard not to be rejected that sometimes we reject ourselves in the process. At twenty-eight years old I remember Marie, a friend of mine, looked me straight in the eye and said, "Rhonda, you work so hard at pushing people away, but then you have to work double hard to win them back." And it was true. My "friendships" lasted about a minute. I was so scared to be rejected that I rejected first. I would "decide" that I didn't like you, and then if that didn't bother you, I liked you. What wasted energy!

My fear of rejection was in charge. It decided who I would be friends with and who I dated. I acted so tough, pretending rejection was par for the course. It didn't bother me, I assured myself and anyone else close enough to listen. In reality I was craving love, affection, and attention. But I was afraid that if I showed that part of myself, I would be vulnerable (a dirty word if you don't want to be rejected), i.e., look weak and be rejected for sure. So, I figured out a plan that if I rejected first, then only the ones unaffected were "worthy" of my friendship. Of course, they were the very ones who were as unemotional as I was and, in truth, unwilling to admit they were human. They ended up being the worst of friends.

The greatest gift I have given myself is the realization that I am human. I have feelings. I am not perfect. My drive to avoid rejection was my desire to be superhuman. If I could get past what most mortals fear, I would be special. That yearning for specialness kept me stuck.

When I was willing to face my humanity I had a chance. Being human gives me the opportunity to be true to myself. It allows me to have feelings without the fear that something is wrong with me. It has given me the courage to reach out regardless of potential rejection. I have learned that when I put worth on my own feelings, thoughts, and actions, they can be rejected. But it doesn't mean I am rejected. My thoughts might be. My feelings may be unwanted. My actions may bother someone, but it is not a reflection of my true nature. I have learned that it is better to be rejected than compromise who I am and reject my true self.

Rejection is going to happen because all of us have varying opinions, values, and beliefs. When someone is supposedly rejecting you, it is not you they are rejecting. It is your values, beliefs, opinions. I know that it feels personal. Being objective during these times of emotional upheaval will support you in seeing the truth of rejection. The act of rejection says more about the person rejecting than it says about you. It tells me what they fear, what bothers them, what pushes them to react.

Mona was deathly afraid to get rejected. She rarely dated and had few friends. She came to see me because she wanted to fall in love but couldn't get past the hurdle of dating.

"I believe in love at first sight," she exclaimed. "I think if a man wants me he should come and get me. I have an eight-year-old and I don't want to bring a man into her life unless he is going to stay there forever."

Mona was asking for a huge commitment right at the beginning and expected a man to know how he felt from the get-go. It was a tall order that I was sure would be unfulfilled.

"Mona, what if you had to date five men before you found Mr. Right?" I inquired.

"Impossible. I can't do that. That means five men might hurt me or betray me or leave me. And, Rhonda, I really believe I will know if he is the right one immediately."

I asked Mona to meet me at the local mall later that evening to conduct a survey about couples in love. She thought that was a great idea and was confident that her findings would be validated.

We created a list of questions, including things like: how did you meet, was it love at first sight, how did you know you were in love, were you friends first, when did you know it was forever?

As Mona approached couples, she heard some startling facts. Rarely did a couple know they would end up together when they met. Usually it took time for them to get to know each other before they fell in love. Most of them met through friends or a work-related event and became friends first. They had dated several other people before they met. On average it took the couples several months before they became a couple.

To put it mildly Mona was shocked. Finding out that her beliefs kept her alone was a revelation for Mona. Learning that rejection is part of the process of intimacy, Mona began to date, giving up her expectations of forever to get to know somebody right now.

Rejection is unavoidable. It cannot be evaded if we take risks and break boundaries. If you want success, you will face rejection. I, as a creative person, must be willing to be rejected for my thoughts, words, and deeds if I want to share my point of view with the world. If I took actions that avoided rejection, I would also avoid success. I would not speak or write or coach. I would people-please and agree. I would feel frustrated and unsatisfied. I would be stifling who I was.

I must be willing to be rejected if I am going to be an individual with my own thoughts, taking actions based on my personal commitments (rather than my family's or society's) and living the life of

MY dreams. The key word there is *MY!* But how often do we stop our-selves (rejecting who we are) from moving forward on our OWN ideas because it may, potentially, make someone else uncomfortable, upset, or disappointed? How many times do we judge our own creativity against another's? It is OUR creativity. Period! How can we compare something that is so unique? Yet, we do . . . rejecting our talents, ideas, and values every step of the way. And when we do that, we are rejecting ourselves and putting our ultimate success on hold.

To be willing to risk sharing all of you, in order to know you are loved as you, is the greatest gift you can give yourself.

Rejection is a fear that must be faced if we are to realize our full-ness as individuals. I understand it may not be pleasant or wanted, yet the mere act of trying to bypass it causes it to grow. As the fear of rejection looms larger, our hearts close up and our eyes shut to the world around us. Beauty fades and we lose hope.

Risking rejection is saying yes to life. It proves that you believe the universe is a magical place to live. It shows the world that you have hope and that love is worth the risk.

I experienced that when I finally faced my fear of my father's re-jection. After my father shot my mother and killed himself when I was fourteen, my father's spirit was always lurking around my closet. The minute my head hit the pillow, the nightmares would begin. They were always the same: my father chasing me through the woods, using me as target practice.

Most nights the bullets would pierce my body. Exhausted, I would wake up feeling like I had been in a war zone. My body would ache with pain and sometimes, I swear, I could literally feel bullet holes in my back or through my heart. And each day the sun would rise I would feel torn—on one hand glad to be alive and, on the other, dreading the day, knowing I would have to face the night. I never told a soul about my nightmares, convinced they would think I was crazy.

For years I would sleep with the light on, hoping that if it worked against vampires, it would keep him away. But it didn't. Each night he would enter my dreams and turn them into nightmares. As I got older, I found alcohol numbed the nightmares. Sure, it produced hor-rific headaches, but it was better than facing my father night after night alone. Yet once again it proved to be ineffective, so once again I woke up wondering why he wouldn't leave me alone.

My father never did like me. His rejection was a constant in my life. Twenty years after they died, my mother's best friend confirmed the truth everyone had tried to hide from me. She said plainly without being asked, "Each time your father looked at you it was with such disgust." Five years later I read nearly the same thing in a letter my mother had written to my aunt. "Ron [my dad] hates Rhonda so much, I don't know what to do." Another victory for my sanity. Another loss for my soul.

Reading the truth was painful, but it was better than being told the old line that we have all heard: "No, your father didn't hate you. He loved you. He just didn't know how to show it." He showed his love by strangling me at twelve. He showed his love by giving me the privilege of watching him kill my most beloved mother. He showed me he loved me by haunting me night after night even after he was dead.

Fourteen years after his death, as I lay in bed recovering from a car accident, unable to leave my house, my father once again was peeking out from my closet door. No, I didn't actually see him but as always, I felt him. I had quit drinking. I was all alone. And he and I were once again face to face. I attempted to ignore him. That didn't work. I attempted to fall asleep. It was impossible.

And then all the years that he had put me down, ignored me, and ultimately rejected me began to play over and over in my mind. The rage rose within me until I couldn't take it anymore. I shouted out demanding an answer. What was he doing here? Why wouldn't he leave me alone? What did he want from me?

There was only silence. Feeling defeated and once again ignored, I screamed at him to leave me alone. I pleaded and finally begged him to go away. I was nearly at my wit's end. Unable to sleep and unable to drink, I couldn't bear to face one more nightmare. I cried. And then sobbed. Exhaustion set in.

I was spent. I had to sleep, but how? I searched for a new plan. There had to be something I could do, but what? Then a thought came to my mind that was almost inconceivable. If you can't beat them, join them. This revelation, this simple deed, had been unthinkable just seconds before, but now it was clear: It was the only thing left to do. As I surrendered, the thought of forgiving him brought with it a deep calm.

Wiping away my tears, I looked over at my father and asked him to come to me. I didn't know how I would do it, but I had nothing to lose. As he stood right in front of me, I told him I forgave him for all those years he had rejected me. I forgave him for rejecting hope and love when he killed himself and my mother. I told him I understood. And in that moment I did. A wave of compassion moved through me and I asked him to come closer.

I opened my arms wide and then I hugged him. Probably for the first time in my life. I really hugged him. I knew in that moment he did love me and I, in turn, loved him.

As he hugged me back, he whispered in my ear, "This is what I have been waiting for." And with that he was gone.

I could hardly believe it. Could it be that simple? A sense of peace fell over me and, exhausted, I fell asleep.

That night the nightmare started the same. My father was behind a low stone wall, firing in my direction. I was shooting back from behind a large tree not more than fifty yards away. We exchanged gunfire for a few minutes, and then I did something I had never done before. I didn't turn and run away but instead stepped out from behind the tree and faced him, throwing my gun down on the ground.

"Go ahead and kill me if that is what you want. I am through." And I spread my arms out so he would have a good, clean shot. Death didn't scare me anymore. I just wanted it over.

He fired. Missed. And then fired some more. As each bullet missed me, he became more and more agitated. He loaded his gun and fired with new determination. But after several rounds he was clearly perplexed. He couldn't hit me no matter how carefully he aimed.

In that moment he put down his gun and exclaimed, "I guess that is over. Do you want to have a picnic?" And with that he came out from the behind the wall, carrying a red-and-white-checkered tablecloth and a picnic basket loaded down with food.

When I was willing to face my father once and for all, face the fear of being rejected once again, my nightmares stopped. Rejection is a powerful force that can either stop you from living or propel you forward. When I finally felt like I had no choice, that I could no longer reject my feelings or deny the experience, I had to face it.

Be willing to face your fear of rejection. It includes a gift of courage to be your true you. When I was willing to love my father despite his rejection, I won. I was set free. Love anyway. Give compassion anyway. Risk anyway. Don't let rejection win.

Today, Risk Rejection

Being willing to risk rejection on a daily basis will catapult your life forward. The fear of rejection keeps us frozen and inactive, when speaking up or asking for help would be the fearless steps to take. Let's find out more about how you handle rejection and where it exists in your present life.

Today, pay attention to the way you handle rejection in all areas of your life.

Do you feel rejected at work? Home? Creatively? From yourself?

When you feel rejected, how do you react? Get defensive? Shut down? Get angry?

When, where, or with whom are the feelings of possible rejection most likely to occur?

What other ways could you deal with rejection? Come up with five new ways to deal with rejection that empower you.

1.
2.
3.
4.
5.

Learning to understand how you process potential rejection is an important step in identifying possible solutions. It is difficult to remember that rejection isn't personal—but it isn't. My father didn't reject me per se, I just happened to be the one he rejected. Rejection can steal your life if you let it. Don't. Master it and you will be mastering fear.

For or Against

Imagine walking into a roomful of strangers. All the assigned greeters for the event are busy welcoming other newcomers. Grabbing your name badge, you sneak by. As you approach the bar, the bartender turns away. You attempt a conversation with the guy sitting next to you but he doesn't answer. How are you feeling? What are you thinking about?

Let me give you two scenarios:

1. The minute you walk into the room you feel alone. No one is there to greet you and you don't recognize any faces. You're convinced that the greeters are unprofessional because they aren't noticing the newcomers like yourself and the others aren't doing their job: greeting you. You grab your name badge and walk in, figuring it has got to get better. But you're wrong. The bartender snubs you as you wave him down to get a drink. He doesn't even give you the time of day. You swear he saw you. It makes you feel invisible. When the guy sitting next to you ignores you, it's the last straw. You have been there a total of ten minutes and you can tell the evening is going to be a complete waste. It is going to be one of those nights. How can one person be rejected by three people within a matter of minutes? You feel like going home.

2. You are excited to be going to this event. You are looking forward to meeting new people. As you approach the greeting table, you notice it is empty. It doesn't matter to you because now you can go to the event and start meeting folks. As you approach the bartender he

turns away; you figure he didn't see you coming. You wait patiently and start up small talk with the guy next to you. You figure the music is too loud for him to hear you. Oh, wait, he is talking to a pretty girl. You want to give him a wink and say good going but you don't want to interrupt. With your name badge on and drink in hand, you start to circulate, trying to meet as many as possible. You feel exhilarated.

Which scenario would most likely be your reaction: scenario one or scenario two? Would you feel frustrated by your lack of connection to others or brush it off? What about if someone turned away from you? Feel snubbed or forget about it, not take it personally— which one is closest to the truth of how you would react with this set of circumstances?

Now, if your answer was scenario one, fundamentally, whether you want to credit it or not, you believe the world is against you. You wait for the other shoe to drop. If someone is nice to you, you believe they want something from you. You have a hard time accepting compliments. If you have some good times, you secretly are waiting for the bad times to hit. Nothing ever lasts forever is your motto. You have a tendency to feel dejected and ignored. In your mind someone is trying to keep you down, whether it is your boss who hasn't seen your potential or your mate who doesn't do their fair share or your mother who won't let you grow up. Overall, life is hard.

If your answer was scenario two, you believe the world is for you. You give people the benefit of the doubt. When good things happen to you, you believe it only proves more good things can happen. A grateful heart is something you have learned to cultivate, and being more loving or compassionate or understanding is important to you. You figure if there is a problem, you can solve it. And you've realized there is no one to blame for your life except you. Your secret philosophy is that dreams do come true.

Most people would want to believe that they think the world is their friend, yet in reality, when the going gets tough most folks act like the world is against them. Listen to the backstabbing and complaining. When you get into a pinch, do you believe the world is fundamentally good or fundamentally bad?

What you focus on turns into your reality.

David was frustrated at his job. At fifty-five he knew what he was doing, but in advertising, youth sells. And he knew he wasn't getting any younger. He was devastated when he was pulled from a major national account because his boss said he wasn't in touch with that market, eighteen-year-old ski bums. Well, he didn't know too many other ad execs who were eighteen and a ski bum.

It felt personal. He always thought his boss was out to get him. As David thought about all the accounts he had, he started to put two and two together. He figured out that his boss just didn't like him.

That was when he came to me. David wanted to quit his job, but at his age he wanted a game plan. He didn't want to be one of his friends, unemployed for two years because he was overqualified.

With two kids in college and a wedding on the way, he didn't have time to play victim. "David, do you believe your boss is for you or against you?" I asked.

His head jerked around so we were face to face. "Rhonda, haven't you been listening? I just said he was against me. I knew my boss didn't like me and now I have the proof."

"What are you going to do with the proof?" I asked.

"Well, I have been thinking about that. The regional vice president would have power to fire my boss, but I think they are in cahoots. I thought about going all the way to the top, the company CEO, but I just don't think it matters to him. I have been racking my brain trying to figure out who I can tell that can solve this problem. But I haven't come up with anyone."

I sighed, praying that he would realize what he was doing before I had to break the news to him. But to no avail. I had to lay it on the line.

"David," I said, "tell me, has anyone else ever tried to sabotage you?"

"That is what I am saying. This always happens to me, so I want you to help me get out of these situations once and for all. I want you to help me deal with these jerks." David was excited at the prospect of finally getting to the bottom of the frustrating life.

"I can help you with that, David. Absolutely," I said.

"Great. Let's start. Tell me what I can do to get this guy out of my life."

"David, I have news you might not want to hear. But I know you want to change your life, so here goes: Your boss isn't against you. You are against you."

"Oh, Rhonda, that is ridiculous. I know what I am talking about." David argued. "I can prove it to you."

"You can!" I countered. "Go ahead."

He went on and on about how one person after another were idiots, like who he'd worked for in the past and the employees who can't get it together. It was a long list of everyone having a problem except David. I let him go on as long as I could stand it.

"David, what is the common denominator in all those events?" I asked.

And that's when it hit him. It was him.

Thinking people are against you never makes you a better person. It doesn't protect you from anything. It doesn't prove you are smarter or wiser or more insightful. It doesn't do anything for you but turn your heart hard. I asked David if that was what he wanted.

"Of course not." He sighed. Underneath his sunny exterior lay a man who believed that he had to fight his way through life. Perhaps not with fists, but with his words.

Many people, like David, profess love but regularly act less than loving. It's not that they don't try. In his own way, putting others down or blaming others was his way of unconsciously making himself feel better. But in reality, as he pointed out another's misgivings he was advertising that he was afraid of not being seen, appreciated, or respected. And those fears gave him permission to try anything and say anything to prove he was okay.

"David, do you think the world is against you or for you? And be honest," I said.

He shook his head, afraid to answer, but he knew the gig was up. He thought the world was against him. He had had no idea. He had always thought of himself as a giving, loving guy.

If I were to describe David after the facts were revealed, I would say he was confused, angry, and lonely. There is nothing lonelier than when you believe the world is against you. I understood. For most of my life I had felt the same way.

After my parents died, many of my friends weren't allowed to play with me anymore, relatives no longer stopped over to visit, and I thought my parents' deaths were my fault. Combine all of that and you have one little girl convinced the world was against her. I knew there had to be something in David's past as well, but that didn't matter. All that mattered was that David wanted to change. He was willing. That's all I needed to know.

Do you plan on life working for you or against you? Do you anticipate people liking you or disliking you? Do you expect life to be easy or hard?

We all have a basic filtering system that either anticipates good or repels good. If you are bent on seeing things from a negative point of view, your filtering system will find a way to make that a reality regarding any situation. That also works for a positive frame of mind. Either way, you win!

If you anticipate good you may be thought of as an optimist, a positive person, one who operates from a sense of accountability and freedom. If you are just waiting for something to go wrong, fear is influential in your choices and plans your results.

The good news is that we are all now adults. We can choose our filtering system. With each decision we make, we are either operating from fear or freedom. If fear is winning, we think we must protect ourselves from the big, bad world and proceed only with extreme caution. If freedom is on top, we anticipate that life works no matter what the outcome of any challenge. We fundamentally believe that life is good and we anticipate each day with excitement, joy, and a sense of awe. We want to live our lives to the greatest of our abilities and do what is necessary to make that a reality.

So think about your latest rash of decision making. Did you anticipate things not working in your favor or anticipate that they would work for you?

Anticipating good can be scary at first because we can never know the outcome at the start. Yet, based on my clients' experiences as well as my own, I have seen that it does work. What have you got to lose but a negative attitude?

Gratitude is the first essential step to claim the innocence needed to see the world is for you. When the world is against you it is very difficult to be grateful, but that is exactly what you must be. Gratitude cures the jaded, overprotective, and defended heart that feels at home in a world that is not friendly. Gratitude helps you see that the world is for you.

Gratitudes are positive statements framed in the present about a person, place, situation, or event. When you are grateful, you are glad of heart, willing, humbled, looking for the gift inside the challenge; you find opportunities where none existed before, and feel connected to the rest of the world.

It is amazing how a gratitude can change your mind. Go ahead and try it. Think of the last time you thought the world was against you. I challenge you to find the gratitude inherent within the problem itself.

Today, I am grateful for _____.

Let's add to the list. I want you to get really good at being grateful, because once you do, it will be hard for you to think the universe is against you. Actually, it will be a rare event. How would your life be different if you no longer had to defend yourself? Gratitudes take us out of being defensive. You will start looking for the good within anything that seems bad. When you can truly be grateful, you are not able to feel like a victim, you will be unable to blame, and feeling isolated will be a thing of the past.

I asked David to give me some examples of his gratitudes. Just like acknowledgments, the more specific you are the better. Here's David's list:

Today, I am grateful for the opportunity to speak frankly to my boss.
Today, I am grateful for the way my job allows me to grow and change.
Today, I am grateful I asked for help about my frustrations with my job.

Now list some of your own gratitudes. Five each day is optimum. And of course, the objective is to think of a gratitude anytime you feel the universe is against you.

Today, I am grateful for _____.
Today, I am grateful for _____.
Today, I am grateful for _____.
Today, I am grateful for _____.
Today, I am grateful for _____.

Congratulations for creating five gratitudes. Now, where are you withholding gratitude? What do you think you shouldn't be grateful for? I dare you to find a gratitude in any and all situations in your life, whether you want to be grateful or not. Practicing gratitude is a skill that will change your life for the better within minutes.

David experienced that for himself just days after he started writing five gratitudes a day in his journal. The first shift was the way he saw his boss. He no longer felt his boss was against him. It was funny when he realized he had been refusing to see the growth potential in the experience.

"When I realized that everything that my boss had said was an opportunity for me to grow, I quit being resentful. After that my boss and I got along fine. He's actually asked me to be on a special committee that is going to be working on a campaign for a world-renowned nonprofit organization. It seems what I do does matter." David was relieved.

Once you realize the universe is for you all ways, always, you will be able to find the seed of truth within every conversation, giving you the opportunity to grow.

Being willing to change your view of the world takes courage. Have the courage today to see the world as "for" you. When the world is for you it is much more fun to be alive, and easier too!

Today, Be Grateful

Finding the good within any experience is true mastery. I ask my clients to think of a gratitude the minute they find themselves complaining or judging someone else. It shifts their focus immediately. Answering the questions below will help give you the perspective you need to change your life.

List three moments in your life where you felt the world was for you:

1.
2.
3.

List three moments when you felt the world was against you:

1.
2.
3.

Please write a gratitude for each of the above moments:

1.
2.
3.

If the world was for you every minute of every day, how would your life be changed?

Knowing you have the power to change any situation will give you the courage to risk each day. Turning the-world-is-against-me into a gratitude is a skill. It is something that must be cultivated and nurtured if you want it to become a way of life. I encourage you to master it. The level of confidence you gain when the world is for you is immeasurable. Be willing to be that confident.

Day 24

What's Love Got to
Do With It?

Love is infused in your desire to do just about anything. Whether you want to change your job, find a new love, or feel better about yourself, love is what inspires you to push past fear and reach for your dreams.

Look at the reason why you picked up this book. You wanted to change your life. What did you want to change? If you looked close enough you would find a call within yourself for more self-expression, which is a form of self-love.

Your yearnings and desires come from wanting to share more of yourself, express more of who you want to be. I believe that everything comes down to self-expression and the acceptance of what we create. That's why it is so hard for some people to be at the same job day in and day out without new challenges. With no new problems there is little motivation to be more creative. And without the insight to see opportunities to express in the sameness of the day, love has little room to take root and grow.

Andrea was not thrilled about her life. She wanted to change everything about herself. In fact, she wanted to be somebody else. When I met Andrea she was determined to find the love of her life. If she did that, she reasoned, life would be better because someone would love her. She could forget about what she wanted and focus on Mr. Right and his dreams. A distraction is what she wanted, but love was what she needed. Or at least she thought it was.

You hear it all the time: You have to love yourself before you can accept love from someone else. Well, that is true and false. True because you would have a hard time believing you are lovable if you don't see it in yourself. False because it was someone else's love for me that gave me the first glimpse that maybe I was worth loving. Sam was the first man I dated when I moved out to California when I was twenty-five. It was a very difficult time for me emotionally. At this point I was dealing with my parents' deaths basically all alone and I was drinking heavily. It was the worst time in my life.

When Sam first told me that he loved me, I balked. Love me, I thought. What, is he nuts? I wanted to believe him. I was aching to hear those words. I had been heartbroken for so long and I was crossing my fingers and praying this one would be different.

Sam refused to give up on me even when I gave up on me time and time again. His love gave me permission to contemplate what it would mean to love myself. Before that experience I would have thought it was selfish. He was what I needed in order to realize that I did want love that would last. But if love was going to last, I had to face my fears about what it meant to love.

Sam and I eventually broke up but not before I understood I was the problem, not him. It all came down to self-love. Sam was my role model. When I became impossible to handle, he finally realized love isn't enough and said good-bye. I was devastated and tried to blame him for everything, but now, looking back, I can see he was not a bad lover or selfish bastard or jerk. He was loving and kind and good. But I was so insecure that he had to leave me if he had any self-worth.

Sam tried to wake me up to the fact that I hated myself. He could see that somewhere inside of me I had decided I didn't deserve love, so I did what any undeserving person would do, I sabotaged it. I rationalized I was trying to see if he really loved me when I requested ridiculous feats of love. And in the end he chose himself over me. I was secretly thrilled that he cared enough about himself to leave. Sam changed my life when he dumped me.

I have come to realize that my inability to accept Sam's love was only a reflection of my inability to love myself. Who wants to really admit they don't love, let alone like, themselves? I didn't, that's for sure. Lies are always better than the truth when you don't like yourself.

Learning about self-love became a must. I didn't want my father to be right. He had never loved me like I'd hoped a father would, and now I was feeling the same way about Sam. I knew I was making it up. I had to figure this love thing out in order to accept love from another, no matter how much I wanted to deny that anyone could love me.

The question become clear: Was I worth loving? I had to find that out for myself before I could accept that the love from anyone else was real. The same was true for Andrea.

To start Andrea and I had to practice loving acts toward ourselves. We didn't actually believe we loved ourselves yet, but we had to start somewhere and "acting as if" is a powerful exercise that helped us do just that.

I asked Andrea to "act as if" she loved herself when she answered the following questions. Andrea had an opportunity to step into the shoes of an Andrea who loved herself. You do the same.

I realized I was starting to love myself when _____.
My most important act of self-love is _____.
Learning how to _____ is a loving act.
I am worth loving because _____.
I like myself when I _____.
I am no longer afraid to _____.
My favorite quirk of mine is _____.
I _____ daily to remind myself of my worth.
Loving myself is a gift because _____.
My ability to appreciate myself has taught me to _____
_____.

Andrea realized she had started to love herself when she didn't beat herself up when her boyfriend broke up with her. Her important act of self-love was giving herself compassion. She has been learning how to put herself first as a loving act. And she realizes she is worth loving because she actually enjoys her own company now. She isn't afraid to be alone anymore. Having a relationship is no longer filling a need, it has become a choice. Andrea has truly learned to like herself and to appreciate her quirks and uniqueness. Having taken to walking with a friend as a daily gift to herself, Andrea is feeling better than ever.

For the next twenty-four hours, "act as if" you appreciate who you are. Be loving to yourself, and that might include being compassionate, eating healthy foods, saying no, forgiving yourself, taking a bath, calling a friend. Do a minimum of five self-loving acts.

Practice is the key that unlocks the door to self-fulfillment.

To help you keep it up, I have started a list of loving acts. Please add to it until you have come up with a hundred. Focus on things that are loving to you. For instance, taking the time to knit may relax you and therefore be a loving act, but someone else may need to run five miles to help them be true to themselves. Do not write down things you think you "should" do or think you "must" do. Acts of self-love are based on what works for you.

How to use the list: When you are being unloving toward yourself, STOP! Take one of the following actions immediately to shift your frame of mind and remind yourself that you are worth loving. If you are having trouble, get support. Ask a friend to help you stay true to yourself.

50 Self-Loving Acts

1. Say no and mean it
2. Give up being right
3. Let go of your resentment
4. Forgive yourself
5. Call a friend and vent
6. Take a bubble bath
7. Walk in nature
8. Start a hobby
9. Make a sandcastle
10. Cry on a loved one's shoulder
11. Ask for help
12. Hit a pillow
13. Pray
14. Meditate
15. Set a beautiful table
16. Cook your favorite meal
17. Wrap yourself in an afghan
18. Get a pedicure
19. Type a love letter to yourself
20. Listen to uplifting music
21. Visit the zoo
22. Take a two-hour lunch break
23. Go out dancing
24. Celebrate for no reason at all
25. Dig in the garden
26. Get a massage
27. Learn to sing
28. Flirt
29. Smile all day long
30. Go to a comedy club
31. Wake up to soothing music
32. Eat some fresh fruit
33. Call a long-lost friend
34. Learn a new language
35. Light scented candles
36. Display photos

37. Create a photo album
38. Hire a cleaning company
39. Give yourself a gift
40. Write thank-you letters to your friends
41. Throw a party
42. Have an intimate dinner party
43. Plan a vacation
44. Take a dance class
45. Go away for the weekend
46. Acknowledge yourself
47. List your assets
48. Pay your bills
49. Drink water
50. Hum a tune

Another loving act you can do for yourself is called venting. Vent when you have feelings that are bothering you, things that you don't want to feel or know how to handle. Venting is the process that gives you permission to honor your feelings yet encourages you to act on your commitments.

I never vent to the person I am frustrated with or angry at because that isn't the purpose of venting. When you are expressing your feelings, do it with someone who will give you the space to have your feelings but not judge you for having them. It is an opportunity to process your feelings under the loving eyes of another.

Ask a friend to listen and listen only. No coaching or advice, please. And let your feelings out. Tell your friend everything that is bothering you. Don't be looking for the answer yet. That isn't what venting is about. It isn't about fixing the problem. Venting is about clearing the air, processing your feelings so you can gain clarity of mind in order to eventually make a powerful decision.

So when you are venting, remember a friend's role is to support you while you are experiencing feelings that you need to process in order to gain clarity of mind. When you have the freedom to talk matters through with a listener who will not get caught up in the story, you can gain a new perspective, see things differently, and get the frustration out emotionally. When you've achieved some clarity, you can approach, with love, the person you are having the difficulty with. You are now clear about what is your stuff and what is their stuff. And your job is to discuss what is yours. That is all you can change. You can't change anyone else.

Again, venting is a useful tool with which a person can move through fear. As a listener, it is not an opportunity to take things personally or make it about you. Instead it is a chance to learn to hear objectively with compassion.

I challenge you to continue to do a minimum of one act of love toward yourself a day. I know you may not feel like it sometimes, but do it anyway. You will reap many benefits from "acting as if" when you don't believe it, don't feel it, or don't like it. Do it anyway.

Be willing to love yourself a little bit each day and joy will be your reward. When was the last time you felt joy? Inner joy is something, when attained, that is always present, assuring you of a better life decision after decision. Joy is based on something internal, a faith and knowingness that everything is working out for the best regardless of present circumstances.

Happiness is fleeting. Joy is not.

Happiness is usually based on how you feel in a particular moment. Feelings change rapidly. More often than not they are dependent on what someone or something else is doing for us, to us, or with us. If we feel accepted, we are happy. If we feel heard, we are happy. If we feel unimportant or unworthy, happiness disappears in a blink of an eye. If we feel ignored or unwanted, again, happiness flees.

How does one cultivate joy as well as appreciate the state of happiness that moves in and out of our lives? Joy is a muscle that is not contingent on whether you get your raise or feel understood. It is cultivated when we no longer look outside of ourselves for approval but instead seek our own personal "approval" above all others. It occurs when we learn to love ourselves and stays when we learn to be true to ourselves.

How does joy thrive? Well, are you proud to be you? Do you like yourself? Do you think you are a good friend? Do you react or decide your way through life? Is the direction of your day a reflection of your mood? If you are a moody person, you might be someone who depends on happiness and feelings to direct your day. If you are moody, true joy is rarely present. Happiness is mood dependent. Joy is not. Happiness is based in feelings that come and go like the weather. Joy is based in values, principles, and commitments. Happiness is something we all desire but inner joy is ignited when we walk a path true to ourselves. Authentic words, actions, and thoughts breed joy. Knowing who we are, flaws and all, expands our ability to accept joy into our life.

I will pick long-lasting joy over fleeting happiness any day. What do you choose on a daily basis? What do you share with the world? What do you rely on? Being true to yourself is so important for so many reasons and one of the most significant is, it determines our ability to have inner joy.

Self-love is a foundation for inner joy. I know for myself that when I am not up to par, the inner joy I feel from within keeps me positive. It keeps faith alive. It reminds me constantly that nothing can stop me from loving myself unless I let it.

Love is the most precious gift we give and receive. Be willing to cultivate it today, if for no other reason than the pure joy of it.

Today, Love Yourself

To help you dig deeper regarding your beliefs about self-love, answer the following questions. It is imperative that you are as truthful and as thorough as possible. There are no wrong answers.

What would you do differently right now if you loved yourself?

How would loving yourself change your ability to take risks?

If you were true to yourself, could you love yourself better?

How would your life change if you had joyful living as a goal?

Love makes a difference in our lives. I know it has changed mine completely. If Sam hadn't loved me when I needed love most, I am not sure I would be a life coach today. His love was like a rope being thrown out to me when the seas of my emotions were overwhelming me. It would have been easy to drown. Love gave me hope. It showed me that I am worth something and that my love matters. It was a surprising and scary time but one that changed my life. Be willing to change your life today by learning how to love yourself.

For the next twenty-four hours your job is to love yourself. Show yourself compassion and kindness at every opportunity. Give up pleasing everyone. Put your needs above anyone else's for today. Learn to ask for what you want and be willing to be vulnerable. The love you are willing to show yourself today equals the amount of love you have right now to give away.

Day 25

Forget Motivation

Companies want to hire the best motivational speaker they can afford in order to get their sales force moving to improve their quality of service. Motivation is a hot topic.

I have been called a motivational speaker since I began giving talks in 1996. I have never liked it. I take issue with the intent. To motivate means to provide incentive, to stimulate the interest of. Motivation is designed to urge you to take action now. It doesn't necessarily teach you anything that will sustain permanent long-term change. Therefore, you can bet you will once again be unmotivated once the rush wears off. And that is my problem with it.

Motivation is a short-term solution. I think of all the motivational tapes I listened to and the books I read. I would get hyped up and excited about what I was going to do, but I would rarely accomplish it. The consistency was gone because I was waiting to be motivated instead of being proactive. I let my feelings get in the way. Left with the guilt and shame of another failed attempt, I once again tried to convince myself if I only was motivated my life would be better.

I had the perfect excuse: my feelings. My feelings got in the way of my motivation. Do you see why I don't like the word *motivation*? Until I gave up trying to motivate myself, I did not realize it was my shaky commitment that was standing in the way. Motivation is like inspiration; it is an effect. It is not the cause.

Jackie was an artist who was having an artist's block. Forty years old, she had been creating impressionistic art for over a decade. She was no longer inspired and that had been her sole motivation. Inspired by a word or a color or an object, Jackie could create something never seen before. She was stuck and had three projects due in the up-coming month. It was crunch time. She wanted to be "cured" of her problems and she wanted miracles now. There is huge difference be-tween demanding a miracle and preparing for one.

"Inspiration is not the cause of your art," I explained. "It is the ef-fect." I went on to tell Jackie that as an artist who works only when she is inspired, she could blame the lack of inspiration for her fail-ure to create. I had to break the news to her. It wasn't inspiration's fault. It was hers.

"Do you get inspired when you work with colors or textures?" I asked. She nodded her head. That was just what I wanted to hear. I dared her to do the following. Take a color swatch or a fabric sample and begin to copy it.

Jackie interrupted. "I don't like to copy," she explained. I was not asking Jackie to copy, I was asking her to start copying in order to get her paintbrush moving. Through my work with creative people I have noticed that when they begin to work in their medium, regard-less of their mood, they inevitably would become inspired. The very act of creating inspires us to create. If we do not create, we will not be inspired. Inspiration is the effect. Willingness and application are the cause.

The same goes for motivation. Motivation is the effect. Commit-ment is the cause. If you are committed, you will be motivated. Feel-ings do not decide commitment, and more often than not they destroy it.

As humans we have been trained to go for effect, but that is short-sighted and only leads to dissatisfaction. When Jackie focused on being inspired, she did not count on herself to create a masterpiece. Yet, if she would just put her paints to canvas, simply perform the act regardless of how she felt, I guaranteed her she would become in-spired. It is the commitment, the work itself, that inspires and mo-tivates us. It is that which produces miracles.

Think of prayer or meditation. If you pray only when you need God, your connection is not as clear or as strong as it could be if you prayed for all different reasons but, more important, for the sake of prayer itself. The same goes for meditation. If you meditate to get a result each and every time, you will be disappointed. If you meditate as a practice, over the long term it will produce extraordinary results. It is in the willingness to keep our appointments with our commitments (including those to God) that we are able to start seeing how cause turns into effect through our own hand.

What effect are you trying to produce? What results do you want to attain?

Motivation solves problems short-term, but for long-term results you must get to the cause of the problem rather than focus on the symptom. A lack of motivation is a symptom that says fear is in control. When we are afraid, we want to go for the quick fix, but the quick fix won't fix anything in the end.

I don't want you to burn out, I want you to shine bright. Trying to force yourself to get motivated is like trying to drive a car with an empty gas tank. No matter how much you want to get where you want to go, the car isn't going to start.

When Jackie joined a Fearbuster Group she had announced, "I am here to get motivated." But no one can motivate anyone else. Inspire? Yes. Encourage? Yes. Support? Yes. But motivate? No.

My distaste for motivation has come from the countless individuals I have seen beat themselves up, put themselves down, and generally push themselves into a breakdown, all under the guise of motivation. When I hear people say they want to get motivated, I hear: If I were different, if I could just get off my butt, if I had more focus, more energy.

And I have found that when people say they want motivation, what they are really saying is they want to skip the steps necessary to create change from the inside out. Instead, they want to go full force ahead. Now, there's nothing wrong with moving forward with intention, but moving headfirst and leaving your heart behind is not going to get you where you want to go. It will get you somewhere, but not where you probably want to be.

Let's replace the word *motivation* with *commitment*. If you want to get motivated, get clear on your commitments. When you are focused on what matters, it is easier to do what you need to do even when you don't want to. Feelings do matter, yet commitments can help you separate fact from fiction quickly and easily.

Cause and effect. Cause: commitment. Effect: motivation. When you are motivated, life happens, but only if you first get clear on your commitments. Be sure to get your priorities in order. And your actions will cause some great results to happen.

What are you committed to?

When you want to get motivated, it also tells me you are not content. Contentment is the antithesis of motivation. When you are content, it is assumed changing your life isn't necessary. When my client Gary started to feel content about his life, he began to worry. His fears were loud and clear: "This must not be good. I will lose my edge. I won't be as competitive. I must be missing something. This is too good to last. When is the other shoe going to drop? I'd better get motivated."

He wanted to prepare for the worst, so he started working harder and faster to keep his fears at bay. He couldn't relax. He couldn't stay satisfied. He wouldn't put his guard down for one minute because someone would surely exploit, betray, or hurt him. The instant he felt content he had to push it away and focus on getting motivated so he for sure was at the top of his game.

I shared with Gary that, yes, I, too, used to believe that. And then I uncovered the source of those thoughts: my fear of being a loser and worthless. My fear wanted to convince me that resting and relishing in contentment was definitely a no-no. I would hear in the quiet of the night, "You'd better get motivated. Relaxing is slacking."

Gary was afraid to be seen as a failure, so the thought of being content brought up all his fears about why failure would happen for sure. He was stuck in a cycle of perpetual motivation. He was exhausted.

What could Gary do to stop his fear from running his life? He had to do exactly what he dreaded most. Relish his success. Enjoy his downtime. And be willing to let go of any sense of future doom. Be present with where he was and give himself permission to feel content.

Contentment is being satisfied. And when you are truly satisfied you still continue to grow and expand. Because you want to keep expressing, not because you'd better or else. You no longer push yourself to be more. You are fine just the way you are. And yet you are open and available for any opportunity that comes your way.

I am not talking about settling or compromising. Contentment is about being grateful for what is and being willing to break through any limitation. Acknowledging what you have accomplished and knowing that more good is on the way.

Not yearning for more but being willing to accept more. Not needing to prove yourself anymore but wanting to be the best you can be, not for others but for yourself.

Gary and I worked through his fears of self-acceptance. He was one of the folks who believed contentment was death. That was the key I needed. I shared the stretch/risk/die formula to give him perspective on how courageous he was already. Now it was time to enter the die zone and be willing to work on contentment.

I asked him to define contentment. You do the same.

Define *contentment:*

Can you be content? Can you take yourself off the treadmill of success for five minutes today and relish the life you have created right now? Can you give yourself permission to pat yourself on the back and relax knowing you have done what you can with what you have and that is enough? Is it okay to be who you are?

Contentment cannot be obtained through degrees or promotions or money. Contentment is an inside job. It comes from being willing to like yourself not for what you do but for who you are.

Contentment without an ability to deal with loss is impossible. Wins are fun, easy, and joyful. It's easy to feel content when you are winning. Our losses don't necessarily bring those same emotions to the forefront. Usually, when we experience loss we feel angry, hurt, or even depressed. We can feel victimized or, even worse, like a loser. That doesn't make us feel good about ourselves. Yet, loss is, in fact, a powerfully healing experience. And a necessary step on the road to contentment.

Loss is part of what makes us human. It forces us to grow. It wakes us up. It gives us the space we need to make the necessary changes that will alter our course in life. Loss is one way we are shaped into our greatness.

Each of us, in our own way, has lost someone or something dear to us in our lifetime. Loss can be as simple as the moment we gave up hope, forgot we were valuable, or gave in to avoid a conflict. Loss can be a death of a loved one, a lost promotion, or a dream unfulfilled. Loss can be words gone unsaid, actions not taken, or feelings acted on that were later regretted.

Our regrets point to our loss as well as our anxiousness. We would not be anxious if we did not fear some sort of loss. We would not regret if loss were not part of the equation. Worry is an attempt to avoid loss, yet that is impossible.

Loss is a part of life. Loss can be challenging, exhilarating, or life altering. The key is how you choose to experience loss and how you walk away from it.

In my life I, like you, have lost many things. I lost my parents at the age of fourteen. I lost my love of God at that same moment, only to painfully recapture it many years later. When I got divorced, I lost the dream of a successful marriage and my image of myself as a wife. Last year I watched another trainer facilitate my beloved Fearless Foundation Weekend without me. A deep sense of loss moved through me, as I knew that I was no longer needed the same way I had been before. And all of those losses have been painful—yet they have been freeing.

When I am in the midst of loss, I know it is time to take extra care of myself. It is not a time to berate my choices or my path in life. Each choice we make is the best choice for that moment in time. When loss is present, we now have an opportunity to step back and reevaluate who we are now.

Are we living from our grandest vision of ourselves? What have I learned from this loss? What does this loss represent to me?

No more looking at loss from a "woe is me" attitude. Yes, loss can be painful. Yes, it brings up our fears. Yes, it can tear us apart from the inside out, bring us to tears, and put us on our knees. And what is the problem with that? Our humanity is a gift and our ability to honor it makes us honor who we are.

What if all of that was necessary for you to give up who you think you are for what you could be? What if you started to view loss as a shove in the right direction? What if loss was the answer to your prayers?

What if loss was one of your greatest teachers? What loss have you denied that is standing the way of your contentment and ultimate satisfaction?

The losses I have yet to face are:

It is our commentary on loss that keeps it around longer. Our opinion keeps it in place. When we judge that we "shouldn't" have loss in our life, in that moment we give up being human and become robots. We expect perfection, yet that is unattainable. Our high expectations of ourselves are the source of much of our pain, our anguish, and where fear runs amok.

The beauty of being human lies in our uniqueness, which can be defined as our gifts, our quirks, or what makes us "different." Loss helps us uncover what is important to us. It points the way to our values and priorities. Loss is one way we find ourselves.

Therefore, loss, ultimately, is good.

Your desire to become more motivated is a sign that your internal life needs support. Loss is present yet denied. You have judgments about who you are and frustrations about life. Things are probably going too slow for you and contentment is out of reach. Being motivated isn't the answer. The answer is defining who you are and following your own path.

The need for motivation is thwarted passion. Let it out. No longer be afraid to express who you are. Be willing to experience and honor the losses that make you you. Your uniqueness, like mine, may have been shaped by your loss. Forget motivation. It isn't the answer. You are. Your true loving self.

Today, Court Contentment

Contentment is the driving force behind our internal satisfaction. Your job today is to court contentment. Examine your life for moments of contentment that support you in trusting, caring, and loving—with the ultimate goal of being true to yourself. Finding your true self lies in those moments. It is where you are at your best and most free to be all of you. Answer the questions below.

What am I trying to gain when I want to become more motivated?

If I were content, what would happen to my passion and purpose?

What loss have I been denying that stands in the way of my being content?

What do you think the connection is between motivation and contentment?

When you find yourself saying things like "Get going. You're not fast enough. Come on, loser," you are trying to motivate yourself through negative self-talk. It won't work. Stop. All you are doing is lowering your self-esteem and your ability to take risks. Instead, ask yourself: Where does contentment lie? What would I have to give up in order to be content? It might be judgment, or a loss that you refuse to give up.

For the next twenty-four hours court contentment. Nurture that part of yourself that is satisfied. The more satisfied you feel, the more you will be moved to honor your true nature and accept it wholeheartedly.

At the end of the day, list your top five most contented moments. Be sure to acknowledge your willingness to notice and nurture them today.

1.
2.
3.
4.
5.

Congratulations. Your ability to be content is growing.

Day 26

Never Confront Again

Jim was having difficulty dealing with Renée, a fellow advertising executive. They had been thrown together to work on a new ad campaign for a sports drink that was being introduced to the marketplace in less than ninety days. Their job was to create a series of print and television ads that would make the drink an instant hit for adults eighteen to twenty-four.

The campaign was touted as revolutionary. At least that's how Jim pitched the idea to the president of the sports drink company. He got the contract but he also got Renée. It wasn't going well.

Renée wanted the campaign to include professional hockey players while Jim thought it was important to have the commercial aim at summer sports. Maybe even have a contest for amateur athletes to compete, with the winner or winners getting to appear in the commercial. They were getting nowhere because they didn't know how to talk to each other.

I had been coaching Jim for about two months when he confessed he had a hard time talking to Renée. He told me she acted so entitled that it made him feel very uncomfortable.

"It always feels like a confrontation, and I don't want to hurt her," Jim said.

"Hurt? How do you know she will be hurt?" I inquired.

Jim went on. "Well, her ideas on the campaign aren't working out and she isn't open to feedback, so I feel like I'm between a rock and a hard place. If I don't confront her about her poor attitude and her ideas, I am afraid we are going to lose this client. And that is my career on the line. I just hate confronting people."

Jim was clearly in a mess but I knew I could help. I asked Jim if he was willing to give up the word *confrontation*. It sounds so abrupt, harsh, and like a battle cry. It doesn't sound like a win-win. It does sound like somebody can't take it anymore. Feeling "used" is a common phrase I hear when it is "confrontation time."

"Well, sure. But that is what it feels like: a confrontation," Jim explained. "I am going to have to go in with my dukes up. You just don't understand Renée. She is impossible."

When two people aren't getting along and are having a bad time communicating, it can feel like an all-or-nothing situation. You are agreeing or you are not. But when you think you must confront, it is always because you don't like the situation as is and want to change it. If it is so terrible, I always ask, why don't you think the other person wants to change it as well? I never get a decent answer.

If Jim wasn't succeeding, neither was Renée.

Confrontation, in my estimation, can bring out the worst in us. If you think you must confront someone, you must feel frustrated, overwhelmed, out of ideas, and that there is little possibility for a solution. Otherwise, why would you want to confront? Couldn't you instead have a conversation? If you feel you must confront, you probably think you are in too deep and are out of ideas for another way. Because shouldn't confrontation be a last resort?

When you are in "confrontation mode," you have lost all inner peace. No one wins. When I feel like confronting someone, I don't want to deal with their problems and be nice anymore. I just want them to understand. I get caught up in name calling and blaming. "They are the problem. I have done all I could" is something I might say. I want to wake them up to the reality of the situation. I can hear myself now: "Are you in dreamland? Get over yourself. I mean it, or something bad is going to happen." Compassion? I have used that all up by this time. When I am "confronting," the problem has become too big for my little mind. I can see no solution. I surmise this is how Jim felt.

I have created a simple solution that I discovered due to my own inability to solve problems by confronting another. It is this: Replace the word *confront* with *clarify*. That's right. When we want to confront, in truth, we want to clarify. There is a missing piece to the puzzle that we don't understand. We are frustrated. We want answers.

I have used this so many times in my own life now that I am sold on it. Whenever I am so upset I can't see straight and am convinced this time I must confront, I stop and tell myself to clarify instead. It works every time.

I just did it yesterday with a coworker. Alisha is one of the producers on the television show I am on where I change people's lives. It started a week ago when I was explaining the next steps I was going to be taking with the client I was coaching, when she got that blank look in her eye. The next thing I know, she is answering the phone and ignoring me. Now, I am sitting right next to her. This happened three more times that day, and finally I had had enough. I wasn't feeling heard or seen or understood. I felt invisible. I had been building evidence all week, watching every move she made, so at the right time, I could say, "Aha, you evil person. I can show you all the ways you were downright inconsiderate and mean. See, I have them listed right here. For instance, you didn't shut the door to the bathroom." (I get so petty when I am building evidence to justify my "confrontation mode.") But you get my point.

I realized what I was doing when I started complaining to another producer about Alisha. Whenever I gossip, I know fear is running the show. It is different if I want to vent and solve the problem, but I had passed that point. I was just complaining to prove my point so I could confront her later.

I clarified instead. There are tons of ways to clarify a situation. I usually ask a question so I can gather more information. It is also a time to defuse feelings. Your job is to get to a neutral place so you can see their point of view. Jim needed to clarify the situation rather than blame Renée for the problem. If he didn't clarify, he was part of the problem.

Let me warn you that in order to have the courage to clarify instead of confront you will be cultivating compassion for yourself as well as another. When we judge, accuse, or blame another, we are ignoring their call for compassion. If Jim had compassion for Renée, clarification would be a lot easier.

I asked Alisha if I could talk to her outside. Confronting or clarifying a potential explosive situation is best done privately. I started off by telling her I wanted to get clear on where we stood.

Could you please clarify that for me . . . ?

Simply asking for clarity gives the other person an opportunity to be heard and an opportunity for you to listen. It will help both of you stop being defensive. Of course, your tone is important. No sarcasm, please.

I don't understand. Could you please use another example . . . ?

Asking for another example is a humbling moment if you are afraid to look stupid or feel inadequate. But it is a great way to disarm the situation and remove the tension.

I'm not sure what you mean by that.

Giving someone the opportunity to explain their position again tells the other party you are listening and want to understand.

What is your intention?

Finding out the intention behind their suggestion or action helps you see that both of you want to arrive at the same place but are getting there by different paths. This is a wonderful way to reconnect through your intentions.

How can I support you?

When anyone is frustrated or upset, they need support. Get off the subject that is irritating both of you and focus on how you can support each other through the process.

Those are just a few ways to clarify in a heated situation. Your job is to pay attention to your tone and be open to hear the answer. If you ask the question but don't really want to listen, they will know it and they will feel manipulated.

And let go of your expectations. Just because you are seeking clarity doesn't mean you are going to get what you want. And we all have hidden expectations. Jim had expectations of Renée and those expectations are what stop us from clarifying. We think they should know, so instead, we get angry and mumble about how we can't believe they are behaving in such a way. Whether you have negative or positive expectations doesn't matter. Expectations by themselves stop us from seeing anyone clearly. They give us permission to feel wronged and, thereby, to confront.

The problem with expectations is they are not usually based in the present. They stem from the rules we have placed on the world based on what someone told us or a previous experience. We expect our boss to be a boss. We expect our spouse to know how we like to be loved. We expect the driver next to us to know how to drive. But who said so?

Expectations limit, confine, and stunt our growth and potential. They place us in a box that is neither comfortable nor fulfilling. They hold us back.

The minute we have expectations, we "think" others (or ourselves) "should" do certain things. Yet, what if the outcomes fail to turn out according to plan? Perhaps your husband told you he would be home by seven o'clock and he isn't. Does that make him a liar? Maybe, but probably not. Individuals usually tell the truth in the moment yet circumstances happen to interfere with good intentions. Does that make us bad people? Rarely. More commonly, we are caught in the web of another's expectations, and disappointment is the result—disappointment is often the result of expectations.

No one can deliver one hundred percent of the time; it just doesn't happen. Life is not here to guarantee us a perfect world. Things change. We tell the truth or make a promise based on one moment, yet events happen in the blink of an eye that can transform our promises into impossible situations. Then we feel guilty or bad about breaking our promise. So much wasted energy!

Aren't you tired of being held up to another's impossible-to-meet expectations? Aren't you tired of forcing yourself to be perfect? Isn't it exhausting expecting yourself to keep promises that are no longer true for you, just because they once were?

Does this mean we drop our obligations? Of course not. But if you have stuffed yourself into a box and you are unhappy, even though at one time you "thought" you wanted to be in that box, it's okay to get out. It is okay to change your mind. It is okay to refocus, redefine your current needs, and get a clearer vision.

Expectations limit our focus, giving us the predictable reactions of condemnation, judgment, and frustration. Oh, and don't forget about disappointment.

What about giving up expectations? What about giving another person a break when things shift and change? What about giving yourself a break? I don't know the details of your life, but I am a different person with different dreams than I was twenty, ten, or even five years ago. If I had told myself that I was not a committed person (i.e., a flake) because I had changed my mind in the past, I would not be who I am today. I would be stuck in the past with a belief about myself that isn't true. I would not be me.

Jim had expectations that Renée should know what to do. That she would have the same work ethic he did and be as invested in the same way. But Jim's expectations kept him stuck in believing confrontation was the answer. In truth, Jim needed to clarify, not confront. He needed to go up to Renée and ask her what her intention was and how he could help. Think about it. If someone is not doing his or her job, or is not open to feedback, do you think they might be scared of something? Maybe they are intimidated or don't feel like their work is good enough. Maybe Renée had a crush on Jim. Heck, I don't know. What I do know is that if she isn't communicating, confrontation won't help. It will only close the door of her heart.

When anyone is driving you that crazy, what they really need, and what you really need, is love. My coworker needed love. Renée needed love. Any time we feel a need to confront, it is because we feel we are not being seen, not being appreciated, not being loved. We all want to be loved unconditionally for who we are, not what we do. It isn't easy living in a world that tries to define who we are by our titles and accomplishments. But until each of us clarifies instead of confronts, we will continue to not be seen or heard or understood.

I did get clarity from Alisha. I told her that I needed to get clear on the rules of the office and establish our boundaries. Her dukes went down. Her posture relaxed. And we solved our problem. It was so easy and I had spent over a week wasting my precious energy trying to prove her wrong and be right. And all I had to do was clarify.

Jim and Renée had the same success. They might not be the greatest partners when working on ad campaigns, but they are learning to work it out and support each other rather than compete. And their willingness to clarify is extending past their professional life. Jim has started dating again and Renée is learning how to meditate.

Today, Clarify

Clarification can take the pain of rejection away. You stop taking things personally. Judgments cease and communication and connection increase. The following questions are here to help you gain clarity about where you are stuck in confrontation mode in your life.

Who are you avoiding?

What questions haven't been asked?

What boundaries have not been clarified or rules explained?

What expectations are you holding on to that validate confrontation?

When you give up blaming and commit to clarifying instead, you will automatically have more love in your life. Learning to take responsibility for the areas you have been avoiding in your life is a key factor in being true to yourself. You cannot change your life if you avoid. You can't be true to yourself if you aren't willing to clarify to find out what is possible.

For the next twenty-four hours, clarify your conversations at every opportunity. It is your day to ask questions and listen. Today, you must be willing to change your perceptions of another. When that happens, you are then free to change yourself.

Day 27

Redefining You

"I hate dating."

Lindsey gave me a litany of reasons why dating just didn't work for her. "There aren't enough quality men. They can't take a woman like me who knows what she wants. They aren't ready for a commitment with me when they are worried about their ex-wife, kids, and their alimony payment." And on she went.

I decided to stop Lindsey and point out a little word that was standing in the way of her and love: *They*. "They" this. "They" that. If only "they" would change. For all the confidence and high standards Lindsey seemingly had, it didn't sound like she had much power over love.

"Rhonda, you don't understand. I have tried to be loving, supportive, caring, and it doesn't seem to work. And unless I know a guy cares for me, I don't feel comfortable sharing my needs and wants. In the end I just feel stepped on, drained, and confused."

"And that's the problem," I said. "You have been trying to do the right things to get Mr. Wonderful to love you instead of practicing loving yourself and being true to who you are, which in turn is the only way you will ever feel truly loved."

I understood Lindsey's frustration with love. It seems most women are caught up in an endless cycle of giving love to get love. But the trick is if you don't let the man in your life know your needs and wants, he cannot love who you really are. In other words, you will never feel loved. Your hidden fears will always be there to remind you that he doesn't know the *real* you. This is where much of our love frustration occurs. We aren't willing to share ourselves until we know they love us; but on the other hand, we don't trust that they love us until they see all of us.

Learning how to practice being yourself is the key to feeling loved and expressing love. And when we are on the threshold of dating for the first time in a while, this is even more critical.

After my divorce it felt like my ex-husband had taken all the love I had, and there was little left for me—or for anyone else, for that matter. I wanted someone to take away the scars my marriage had left on my heart. I wanted to be wanted, but there were no men in sight. At least, I couldn't see any.

Losing yourself in love is a hazard in many relationships. We think in order to keep love, we have to keep giving until we have nothing left and hardly recognize ourselves anymore. In my marriage I quit speaking up in order to keep the peace. I had no idea I was giving up a piece of my soul in the process.

When the divorce was final, I knew it was time to contemplate the dreaded pathway to relationships, dating. The uphill battle began. It was my heart against my fears of being rejected, used, and betrayed. It soon became apparent that if I was ever going to be willing to be loved, it was time to learn some new skills. It was time to practice being me and, in some ways, defining who I was all over again.

I shared the following story with Lindsey to explain that just because you want something to change doesn't mean it will, unless you do something different.

During a coaching session with a client recently, I pointed to the Kleenex box on the coffee table that lay between us. The box was green. I began to explain that if the Kleenex box was a metaphor about her current dissatisfaction, it was as if she wanted to point to the box and the color would be red. Yet the box was in fact green. And there wasn't anything she could do about changing the color except, of course, to physically alter the appearance by the use of paint, paper, etc. But the reality was, at this moment, the box was green.

I use this story to illustrate what most of us do when we are faced with a situation that we want to avoid, deny, or blame on someone else. She didn't want to face her present circumstances but until she did, her life, and the box, would stay green. She was frustrated because she felt she was stuck in her present circumstances. She didn't see how that could change, but I knew it could. It would just take becoming fearless.

She sat there slumped over, and sighed. "But I have been so positive about it." And that began my dissertation on green versus red and what constitutes positive thinking.

Positive thinking is when you can look at the green box and find the good in it—not try to change it to red. Don't let the color being green stop you from moving forward toward your dream. It might mean changing the way you view green. Instead of seeing green as the problem, it becomes an opportunity to grow. Or it could be an opportunity to practice your creativity or problem-solving ability and be seen as a leader. That green box, guaranteed, is going to build your self-confidence and help you break through your fear.

Most people use wishful thinking and begin their chant, "The box is red, the box is red, the box is red." Yet they do nothing to contribute to the change they desire. They believe that if they only say the magic words enough times and with a positive attitude, the Kleenex box will eventually turn red. Well, it could, but the key is: You would have to do something physically to change it to red! It will not change itself.

Positive thinking is an incredible skill. When used alongside action, nothing is impossible. The key word is *action.* I explained to my client that no matter what she "wished," the box was still green. In order to alter her circumstances, she had first to see the color green. Only then could she actively alter her present experience and turn the color to red. She had to embrace the box as green. Come to terms with it. And then she could brainstorm, be positive, build a support team, find solutions, and so on. But again, first she had to acknowledge to herself the reality of the situation: The green box was a green box.

When you are willing to have that awareness and move into acceptance of the current challenge (I didn't say feel defeated or give up or compromise), you can make the changes necessary with more ease than you would have previously believed.

Remember: It is our denial and resistance that causes us pain, not the event itself. When we accept the facts in front of us, we can see with clarity if we are contributing to the problem. Then we are free to discover new ways to master the situation at hand. We can get our paints out or start gluing bright colored paper on the box or we might find that we've changed our mind and like green. The way we conduct ourselves shows us who is in control: fear or freedom. And the choice is always up to us.

Awareness brings acceptance and that brings a new ability to see beyond the present circumstances with a positive attitude. When we put action behind our positive thinking, it will spur change in our life that seems like magic.

You may have been encountering many green Kleenex boxes over the last twenty-seven days. You have been working hard on redefining who you are and sometimes, I am sure, things have been hard to accept, just like the green Kleenex box was for my client.

It is time to reevaluate and start putting the pieces together again. When I got divorced I didn't know anymore what my favorite food was or if blue was my favorite color. My friends changed. It seemed nothing stayed the same. I am sure you have experienced some of this on your way to finding your true self.

The following questions may seem simple, but please do not just answer them as you would have twenty-seven days ago. I want you to be willing to re-create the you that is occupying your skin. We are going to start with the basics and build up. Think of it as an opportunity to redefine who you are.

I asked Lindsey to tell me her three favorite memories of herself over the last twenty-seven days. In the past, one of Lindsey's favorite memories would have been walking her dog in the park on a cool autumn day or the vacation she took with her nieces to Chicago. Even though they were twenty years younger than she was, she had a blast. I wanted to know what her memories included now. Was it when she spoke up to her boss? Asked a man out for the first time? When she worked out and was so sore she could hardly move the next day?

Lindsey's list included not getting all dolled up for her date with Victor and his compliments about how beautiful she was, going with the flow and having fun on a date at the carnival where normally she would have been uptight about the dirt and bad food, and lastly, how proud she was of herself when she asked Victor out on their first date. She can still remember how tongue tied she got and how foolish she was sure she looked. She learned to have a lot of compassion for men and their dating requests.

For me, risks create memories. Is it the same for you? Please list the top three memories during our journey together.

Your three favorite memories:

1.
2.
3.

Memories create a new vision for our life. Before Day One Lindsey did not have a vision. As we were getting closer to Day Thirty, she wanted to know how to create one for her new life. Most people do not have a vision of what they want their life to look like or what they want to contribute to the world. Some have a vision, yet it is usually not large enough to carry them through the difficult times and keep them focused on where they want to go. Instead their obstacles stop them from moving forward rather than their vision pushing them through.

Vision also has an extra benefit—energy. When you have a vision, energy regenerates itself within you. When you have vision, the vision itself pulls you forward. If you are pulling yourself through, it is your willpower or discipline. If you are being pulled, it is your intuition, your vision, and your purpose pulling you through. When your vision is clear, you don't need motivation or discipline, you *are* discipline because the vision is running the show. Your life is in service to the vision. There is a surrender and acceptance, and in that moment things can happen that would otherwise be prevented because your ego would get in the way. When you live a life of service to your vision, life manifests itself with more ease and effortlessness.

When you have a vision, the process is the key.

I was talking to another coach and she asked me how I wanted to contribute to the world. I told her I didn't. She was shocked.

"What do you mean you don't want to contribute to the world?" she replied.

I explained to her that if I was doing the things I was doing to impact the world, each task would be daunting. It would be overwhelming. What helps me stay centered and focused is doing the next thing right in front of me that needs to be done in alignment with my vision. My job is to help the person before me. If I do that, if I do what is right in front of me, well, then, I know I have done my job. And hopefully, each person I encounter will contribute to the person they touch, and so on. That is my charge.

What is your vision for your life?

Name a movie that best represents your life. Using movies to explain your process is an easy and fun way to learn more about who you are. The way you see yourself through the character you play is an opportunity to rewrite the script.

If you had a sequel, what would it be called?

For years I thought something was wrong with me because I didn't think of the world. Yet, I see that thought defeats me rather than builds me up. Some people need the larger world view to inspire them; it actually disempowers me. So what type of process person are you? What works for you?

What have you learned about how you process information when you are afraid?

What have you learned about how you process information when you are fearless?

Either way is okay. There is no right way to process. Begin to pay attention to what works for you and empowers you. Our journey has included many opportunities to see how you react when you are in fear. Remember stretch, risk, or die? That will help you for years to come when a decision must be made or when you are trying to figure out what is stopping you.

You have processed a ton of information in the past twenty-seven days. That takes a willingness to keep going that is truly fearless!

Let's find out about your friendships. At the beginning of your journey you did or didn't have friends. As you built your skills did your friends change? Are you able to be yourself with your friends?

Who is your best friend now?

Name three people on your support team:

1.
2.
3.

Define what friendship means to you now:

Every time I grow, my friends change. It's as if my friends are in my life for a particular reason and when that reason is gone, they go too! I have few friends who have stayed with me through hell and back. There is my college roommate, Kathryn, and my dear friend Marta. Lisa has been around for a long time too!

Most of my friends have become friends with me since I have changed my life for the better. It is easier to keep friends when you aren't blaming them all the time. And I am a better friend now that I lead with compassion rather than perfection.

What about your job? Does it still suit you? Learning to be true to yourself regardless of your environment is a skill. A skill most people have yet to master, because when we are working our passion is in play and our reputation is on the line. Things become personal.

Have you been able to use your newfound skills at work?

Tell me the top three things you have learned that have supported you in your career:

1.
2.
3.

Please tell me how being true to yourself has affected your career satisfaction:

We spend more time at work than we do at home. We'd better learn to be joyful. And being able to be joyful requires a combination of skills you have learned. Your career is usually the number-one place passion can be expressed and purpose can be revealed.

Now let's go to your home life. For me, home is everything. Even though the Fearless Living Institute has an office, I am rarely there. Instead, I work on my laptop in my living room looking at the view of the mountains and feeling the breeze. There are things in my home that have definitely changed since I have learned how to be true to myself. I hang fall leaves everywhere. Before I would have been afraid of what people would think of my fall motif in the middle of summer, but not anymore. Leaves it is. I love sitting in my hammock, which in the past would have been an indulgence. I am the type of person who can live anywhere, and I do. I live in London part-time when I am taping my television show *Help Me Rhonda* for my United Kingdom audience. Chicago is my present home while I am taping *Starting Over* seven days a week. It is a grueling schedule, so I am rarely home. Yet the minute I hit the door, I pull back the window blinds, open the windows, and look out over Lake Michigan. It brings me back to center. And that is what home means to me. A place to rejuvenate and reconnect.

What does home mean to you?

How has your home life changed since Day One?

What do you want to change but haven't had the courage to?

Learning to see your home as a place to express yourself rather than just a place to lay your head will support you in being true to yourself. It will energize and invigorate you. Take a moment and look around your house. Is there something that has been bothering you? Make a plan to change it. This is your home—allow it to more authentically represent the new you.

We've talked about your friends, your home, and now what about your love relationships. When you change, they must change. There is no way around it. Let's start out with your definition of love. Has it changed?

Define *love*:

How have your love relationships been affected by your commitment to be true?

What needs to change and what skill will help you change it?

If you could tell your mate one thing that you have yet to say, what would it be?

Notice the areas of your life where change has been easy and the others where change is more difficult. Do you know why there is a difference? The more we are invested, the more challenging it is to change.

It is not always easy to be true to yourself, but now that you know what it is like, it is too late to turn back. You are responsible for all you have learned. It is in your heart, mind, and soul whether you are actualizing it or not. It is there. Honor it. It will serve you when you least expect it.

Congratulations on your continued commitment to change your life for the better. You have had some things happen that I am sure shocked and surprised you. That's fantastic. The more we are open to change even the things we think will never change, the more life will be filled with miracles.

Today, Honor Your Growth

Today is the day to honor your growth and reevaluate the changes you have made. We never give ourselves enough credit, so be sure to write down five acknowledgments today for your shifts and changes. Remember to frame them in the positive, write them in the present tense, and be specific.

Today, I acknowledge myself for:

1.
2.
3.
4.
5.

For the next twenty-four hours, honor who you have become. Notice any and all changes. Acknowledge yourself throughout the day to affirm that you are on your way.

Day 28

Beautiful You

D o you want to attract more love in your life? Put more money in your pocket? Be the person people think of when it is time to do anything fun, important, or worthwhile? It is easy. All you have to do is see yourself as beautiful. That is right. Beautiful.

To accept yourself as you are with all of your imperfections is the first step to seeing yourself as the beautiful person you are. Beautiful? ME?! Yes, YOU!

I know you have heard it before, but beauty does really start on the inside. It begins with a commitment to see yourself differently that travels to your brain and finally lands in your heart. From that moment on fear doesn't have a chance. Beauty wins.

Ready to see yourself as beautiful? Ready to see your gorgeous self—radiating out from within? Ready to be a magnet for love, money, and fun? Ready to feel confident, powerful, and passionate? All it takes is a mind shift.

You have been doing the work over the past twenty-eight days. Now it is time to take all of it and apply it to you as a beautiful person. Beautiful people are not petty or resentful. They do not make things up about others. They have learned to accept themselves.

It takes courage to change your mind, to look past the negative self-talk and act from a place that is not marred by fear. It takes a willingness to see something beyond the physical and see the depths of your humanity. It takes a desire to love yourself more than another, knowing in that love you will find the intimacy you crave.

Redefining beauty is the first step. I want to know what you think of when you hear the word *beauty* and how it applies to your everyday life.

Define *beauty:*

What does beauty look like in your daily life?

How would you know when you finally saw yourself as beautiful?

Beauty goes beyond the mirror. In fact, beauty has little to do with the way you look and it has everything to do with the way you act. And you, my friend, have control over that.

If you are like most of the people out in the world, you have contemplated the concept of beauty before but rarely, if ever, applied it to yourself. You may have even told yourself once or twice that you are beautiful, but then those glossy magazines and billboards get in the way. Daily, we compare ourselves to the latest version of perfection splattered, it seems, everywhere. Do you want to embrace your beauty?

We have been working very hard at changing the way you see the world. We have focused on the aspects and qualities that will support you in being true to yourself. Well, it is time to take all of that inside stuff and apply it to the outside. You are beautiful.

So what is beauty? You are beautiful when you accept yourself fully, when confidence and risk taking are your calling cards. It is when you see through the eyes of love rather than fear. When you willingly bare your soul, your beauty shines through. The moment you are open-hearted, vulnerable, or feel exposed, that, my friend, is beautiful.

Willing to risk it all, beautiful people give all. They aren't in it for the outcome but for the challenge, the invitation from their soul to participate in this thing called life. When you fully invest with no guarantee of return, driven by passion and purpose instead of obligation, and keep your own counsel while knowing a wise person always seeks support, that's beautiful.

Truly beautiful people know that a broken heart is nothing to fear but something to court. I understand that this may seem tough. It feels like our commitment to own our beauty pushes and pulls us. And it does force us to walk that delicate balance between our daily desire to connect and our daily fear of being rejected.

I like to say that beautiful people are centered in their self. They are not selfish or self-centered, rather they are centered within themselves. *Selfish* implies thinking only of oneself. *Self-centered* entails putting yourself at the center of everything. I am sure you know people who fit into all three of those categories.

A client of mine named Melissa was selfish and she knew it. Her needs were more important than anyone else's. If she wasn't happy, she let everyone know. Melissa's best friend, Ally, was self-centered. It was a little tricky to catch on to her need to be the center of action because she didn't automatically say, "Me, me, me." She fulfilled her core need of wanting to belong by turning all the conversations into opportunities to talk about herself.

For example, Ally wouldn't complain about her friend, "Melissa is so selfish." Instead she would say, "I would never be so selfish," thereby bringing it right back to her. Folks who are self-centered are harder to spot than those who are merely selfish because they spark conversations and put their needs up front. Theirs is a subtle form of manipulation and they are experts at bringing everything back to themselves. In this case Melissa referred everything back to herself. If you told her you had a cold, she would be telling you a story about the cold she had had that put her in bed for three weeks. If you talked about your latest boyfriend, she would moan about hers, or at the very least compete with you about who had the best boyfriend.

Eva was a client who wanted to leave her selfish ways behind and become what I call centered in self. When you are centered in your self you are not easily manipulated or distracted. Your intuition is your guide. Friends support you, yet they are not your life. Beautiful people are centered in self.

How does one embrace being beautiful? Let me give you three easy tasks that you can perform today that will help you embrace your beauty. They may seem simple, but if you do them with clear intention to focus on the beautiful you, changes will happen and you will begin to be affirmed for your transformation. Practice these skills that will help you become more confident, thereby increasing your beauty quotient.

1—Smile
There is nothing like a smile to give people the feeling that all is right in your world. We all want to be around people who are happy because we want either to stay happy or get happy. A smile is one of the simplest and most effective confidence boosters as you are building internal confidence. Challenge: Smile whenever you greet someone.

If you smiled today at everyone you meet, how would your life change?

2—Read the daily newspaper or a magazine.
A feast of information for daily small talk with strangers, casual coworkers, or potential friends. A little knowledge of your local area can give you a big confidence boost because it gives you something to talk about with just about anyone. No more lack of conversation. It's all in the headlines. Challenge: Initiate one conversation a day with a stranger.

Becoming more knowledgeable about the world around you supports growth. If you took the time to read a newspaper or a magazine or the latest news on the Internet, how would you feel about yourself?

If you feel more knowledgeable, how will that change how you interact with others?

3—Ask questions

Most of us are afraid to look stupid, inadequate, or insignificant. When you ask questions you are building your confidence twofold: With each question asked you are taking a risk (a necessary ingredient to true confidence) of your fear coming true, and you are admitting that you want to learn more or are just plain interested. When you are willing to ask a question, no matter what it is, it tells the world you can handle input and are open to new perspectives and interested in the world. That all points to a strong sense of self. Challenge: Ask three questions today.

Being able to ask questions uses all the skills we have talked about up until now. Being willing to engage another in conversation speaks to your ability to go first in life.

If I asked questions today, how would that affect my life?

•

Practicing those skills, and all the skills that you have worked on in the past twenty-eight days, takes a commitment to excellence, not perfection. Perfection denies your growth. If you are trying to ask the perfect question, you will be stilted. Perfection precludes connecting because it keeps you focused on yourself. When being right is more important then being human, you are being undermined by your desire to avoid the inevitable mistakes. Perfection or connection? Your choice. You can only have one or the other. Because if you connect through your perfectionism, you are presenting a false idea of who you are. A commitment to excellence, on the other hand, supports connection. In order to have excellence you most likely need help.

Excellence allows you to reach out, while perfectionism keeps you hidden within.

Define *perfection:*

Define *excellence:*

A commitment to a life of excellence is a commitment to being true to yourself. And when you are being true to yourself, you are beautiful. You may not know it yet but the world sees it.

How do you know when you have achieved true beauty? You already have. The only thing that stands between you and claiming yourself as beautiful is fear. Fear convinces you that there is no way you can be those things or have them. Fear wants you to doubt yourself, and in that way it controls your every action, every thought, every relationship. Fear sees your beauty and fears its power. It wants to stay in control at all costs and therefore has you consistently seeing through the eyes of fear rather than the eyes of truth, freedom, and love.

To claim your beauty it often helps to think of yourself as you would your best friend. We invariably judge ourselves harshly. Start looking at yourself in a new way: from your warm heart, not your critical brain. Wrap your arms around yourself and hug yourself. Tell yourself you're lovable, worthwhile, valuable—think of the things you like about yourself. Maybe you're funny, kind, laid back, compassionate—whatever. Loving yourself is essential to thinking yourself beautiful.

Now practice accepting yourself as you are with all your perceived physical (and other) imperfections. This will be a sign that you are willing to see all of you and love it. Remember: Look at yourself with the eyes of love, not fear. Look in the mirror and note one attractive thing about yourself—from long eyelashes to well-shaped nails, pretty ears to neat knees. You get the idea: Then do the same thing every day, looking at a different characteristic. You will soon be able to see more than the things you dislike, because your perspective will change. Whenever you are feeling low about yourself, repeat the exercise. It is time to quit blaming your body for your life. Taking care of the outside supports your inside.

If it seems hard, even impossible, to get past the images in glossy magazines, just remember they are constructs. Sure, there's a woman underneath there somewhere, but she has been primped and preened and posed within an inch of her life—and then any imperfections have been airbrushed out of the finished picture. That's not real life. If you use magazines to compare and compete, you are from here on banned from reading them. Banned!

Kim was one of the most beautiful women I have ever met. She was kind, loving, creative, and adventurous. Her family life was the envy of all. Her good-looking, Harley-Davidson–riding husband, who had made a killing in real estate but sang in a band on the side, was a gem. With two children and her own career she was busy. But Kim did not see herself as beautiful. She couldn't even look at herself in the mirror.

I banned her beauty magazines. It was difficult at first, because she had used them for so long to give herself tips to fix her flaws. She wanted to be wearing the trendy clothes and have the latest accessories. I told her she could go to the store and get that advice and talk to a real woman.

Her assignment each day included looking at herself in the mirror and finding one positive thing to say. Being specific helped her get focused on something. The first thing she complimented was her eyebrows. And not both, just her right one. I'll take it. You have to start somewhere. This exercise continued for over three weeks before she found that she could look in the mirror and no longer break into a cold sweat. It took another three months of daily validations before she could stand naked in front of the mirror and say, "I am willing to accept you," without throwing up.

Kim was willing to do this challenging work because, as she said, "I don't want my daughter to feel about herself the way I do about me." And she cried. Six months later that statement was no longer true. I remember the coaching session as if it were yesterday. We were discussing her willingness to accept herself, flaws and all, when she looked up at me and said, "I looked in the mirror yesterday and for the first time in my life I didn't think I was ugly."

It was a breakthrough. She was starting to see what the rest of the world knew. She still wasn't ready to claim beautiful, but for her it was a start, a great start.

When you look in the mirror, what do you see? What do you say about yourself? What if what you said about yourself perpetuated negative thoughts? Kim was willing to be uncomfortable for many months. It seemed useless so many times when she looked in the mirror to repeat her exercise. But it wasn't. Nothing is useless. Are you willing to see your beauty as Kim did?

If I knew I was beautiful, my life would be:

Practice seeing others as beautiful despite all of their fears. Practice seeing yourself daily as the vehicle for the expression of beauty on the planet. Practice redefining beauty moment by moment. Fear will convince you that this won't work. Fear will convince you this is wrong. Fear will convince you that this is stupid. Fear will want to convince you to stop this. Do not listen. Fear is being afraid that you will be hurt, disappointed, rejected. Fear does not want you to know how beautiful you are. But it is too late. You have now tasted what beauty feels like and how it can appear in your life. Go for it.

I invite you to be the beauty that you yearn to be. I challenge you to uphold the quality of being Beauty. I urge you to cultivate the Beauty qualities that are already within. Look in the mirror and point out one of your best characteristics each day. Rub scented lotion on your body and affirm: I am Beauty. When you are kind, loving, or compassionate, affirm once again: This is Beauty. "I am now willing to express the beauty within."

Allow your beauty to shine, and in that moment of willingness you shall see it for yourself. Shine, my beautiful, beautiful friend. Shine!

Today, Be Beautiful

Learning to see your beauty will give you more confidence to be true to yourself. It takes courage to do this delicate and vulnerable work, but it is necessary if you are going to claim all of you.

List five moments when you were able to see your beauty today. I understand it may have lasted only for a second, but to acknowledge that you were willing to see it for that long is the beginning of seeing it as a reality every day.

Beautiful Moments:

1.
2.
3.
4.
5.

As you embrace your beautiful moments, you are claiming the truth of who you are. Look around you. See the beauty. I would like you to list five beautiful images you noticed, people you met, or experiences you had today.

1.
2.
3.
4.
5.

Being able to see beauty in everything you do and everyone you meet will support your seeing beauty within yourself. And being beautiful is a gift that was given to you by your Creator. Honor it.

Do you believe you are capable of seeing your beauty?

If you claimed you were beautiful inside and out and believed it, how would your life change?

What thoughts or feelings come up for you when you contemplate yourself and beauty in the same sentence?

What beautiful things about yourself can you claim now?

For the next twenty-four hours every time you look in a mirror, affirm, "I am willing to see my beauty today." Every hour on the hour say it to yourself silently or write it in longhand in your journal. Being willing is the first step in accessing your beauty.

Day 29

Heaven

The other day I overheard a group of women talking about heaven. One of them had read a book that went into descriptive detail about what heaven looked like and what you did once you were there. They were all fascinated. I wasn't. I have no desire to wait for heaven until I am turned to ashes. Not me. I want to experience heaven every day while I am alive.

But how do you do that? How do you experience heaven while your eyes are wide open and your heart still beats? I can only tell you what I have discovered, and that is heaven is a state of mind. It is when I am being true to myself. When my thoughts, actions, and feelings are aligned. It is the ability to stay present in each moment, deriving from it the pure pleasure of being alive.

But let's face it, how many times can you look at a daisy and experience its wonder? How often do you stop and admire a cloud formation with awe? When was the last time you said thank-you to the stranger who God-blessed you after a sneeze? It can be challenging to stay in the moment and remember all the good in the world.

We can all get caught up in moving faster and having more. I can get caught in it as well. Last week I saw the most beautiful sand-blasted glasses. Each one had a unique leaf design. I couldn't take my eyes off of them. Okay, I was drooling. I had to have them.

I am a huge leaf collector. On my coffee table in my living room I have a basket filled with fall leaves I have carefully ironed and saved over the years. On almost every wall in my kitchen and dining room there are paintings, plates, or pictures of fall leaves. My entire home is the palate of fall. You get the idea. While I was growing up in

Minnesota and Michigan, the fall season called to my soul. So, here I am with leaves in every room reminding me of home.

I glanced at the price tag. Those glasses would be an indulgence. I paced back and forth for over an hour. Justifying the purchase in my mind, I began to calculate my budget for the month, deciding if they were "worth" it. As I began to nickel-and-dime myself to death, I stopped and looked over at the glasses. I picked one up and felt the weight and touched the pattern of the leaves so beautifully sand-blasted. I put away my fear-filled thoughts and just enjoyed the texture and the feeling of home they elicited within me. I was in heaven.

I bought six glasses. Each one had a different design, yet all reminded me of the leaves back home. In that kitchen store I relished the pleasure the glassware would give me. I knew I would not take those glasses for granted and would give them to guests as a testament of my love for them and my surroundings.

It may seem silly going through so much trouble for just six measly glasses. Yet that is the point. They weren't six measly glasses. They were works of art. If they had only been six measly glasses, they wouldn't be contributing to my everyday feeling of heaven. I want as much as I can in my environment, within and without, to give me a feeling that all is possible. Each item contributes to the climate of my self-confidence. Each moment pushes me to be more true to myself.

It could have easily been different. I could have walked away rationalizing that I really shouldn't be buying something so frivolous. I could have called myself selfish and self-indulgent and beaten myself up for even thinking about purchasing such expensive glassware, let alone actually doing it. I could have bought them impulsively without thinking the purchase through. I mean, it isn't like I have dinner parties on a weekly basis. Heck, I haven't seen my own kitchen for two weeks. Yet, I knew. I knew that those glasses would give me more than a moment of pleasure. I knew I had the ability to cherish them for as long as they lived within the four walls of my humble home.

Heaven can be drinking water that tastes so good you want more. It can be appreciating the look your children give you when they need help or when they tell you they love you. It could be using dishes you love and glassware you get giddy over. It could be soft blankets on a chilly night. Heaven is right where you are each and every moment. Heaven is when you are being true to yourself. Are you being true to yourself now more than ever? How have the last twenty-nine days made a difference in your life?

Define heaven on earth:

Where do you have a slice of heaven on earth in your life right now?

Let's commit to living a life where being true to yourself is not a once-in-a-lifetime event but a moment-by-moment experience. Let's decide that right now, today, there is no going back. You have been doing the work diligently every day. You have proved that changing your life is more than a "have to," it is a "want to." Heaven exists on earth when you are being true to yourself.

I would like you to read the following out loud. These are some examples of statements of commitment. You will be writing your own at the end of today. Let's begin.

Today I am going to act as if the whole world loves me.

I am going to walk tall and be proud of who I am and what I have accomplished and have yet to accomplish. I am going to speak my mind and believe, with my whole heart, that people love me and respect me and want to hear what I have to say. If someone doesn't see my value, I know they are in fear. In that moment I brush aside any fear of being unworthy. Instead, I am aware that being true to myself is the greatest gift of love I can give to myself.

Today I am going to live as if I can be happy.

I am not going to wait for or expect the other shoe to drop. I am not going to anticipate the worst or focus on the negative comments or condescending faces. Instead, I decide that happiness is my natural state of being and I can be happy regardless of the events in my life. Happiness lives in intention, not in fear. As I am willing to let go of fear, I choose to embrace a happy frame of mind. I give myself permission to have a happy ending.

Today I believe that everything goes my way.

Does it mean I get everything I want? Not necessarily. Yet I choose to trust that I get everything I need. And each step on my journey is moving me toward a more expansive and loving version of myself. As I trust the process called life, I release my attachment to a specific outcome. Instead, I relax and watch life unfold magically. I notice as I give up pushing life to happen, life guides me effortlessly on a path filled with purpose and passion.

Today I am going to smile at everyone I meet.

Even if I am on the phone, my smile will be so big that the person on the other end will know that I am smiling. They will hear it in my voice and sense my inner joyfulness. I know that this will give them permission to be joyful as well. As I smile, I am teaching the world to smile. As I smile, I am telling my body and my mind I am willing to be happy. As I embrace happiness, I am honoring the truth of who I am.

Today I am going to decide to take to heart every compliment I receive.

No longer do I evaluate and judge the compliment by the giver. All compliments are valid. They are a gift and today I accept each one with grace and ease. Pushing them away is fear talking. And fear no longer runs my life. Instead, I attract into my life the best people, places, and situations for my greatest good. As I accept compliments, I am saying yes to life.

Today I choose to be in love.

Today I choose to be in love with the person who has always been by my side: myself. I am going to thank myself for sticking it out through the various trials and tribulations of growing up as well as the heartaches and frustrations. I am going to acknowledge myself for being willing to get up after a fall even though I didn't feel like it. I am going to look myself in the eye and say:

"I love you. Thank you for standing by me. Thank you for be-lieving in me and supporting my dreams. Today, I choose to ac-cept myself fully and be myself fully. I like being me. I commit to being true to myself."

I am going to say that statement to myself a minimum of three times and mean it! I am taking one step closer to truly understand-ing love between two people. As I move closer to loving the parts of myself I may, in the past, have rejected, I am learning to have com-passion for the world at large, for other people, and mostly for my-self. As I take on love as a way of being, instead of fear, I stand for myself, speak my truth, and let the people, places, and situations go that I have been clutching, grabbing, and hanging on to for dear life. I see now that they can't make me afraid, I have been doing it to my-self. I let go and in letting go, I find love in unexpected places. I find love within myself. And in that moment heaven does exist on earth, because I am willing to see that the world indeed loves me just as I am.

Today, I commit to being true to myself.

What was it like to read that out loud? Did it inspire you? Did you feel better or worse about yourself? Writing down your commitments in letter form is a powerful exercise and one that you will be doing later—but for now, tell me how it felt.

When I read the commitment letter, I felt:

This commitment letter helps me be true to myself because:

Giving yourself credit is a theme we have been discussing since Day Two. And it continues to be important in building your confidence and risk-taking ability. After all, everything we are doing together is about taking more risks so you can go anywhere, do anything, and meet anyone.

When you commit to a new way of being, it is time to celebrate. For instance, celebrate your willingness to commit to being true to yourself one more time. It's time to celebrate each step you took toward changing your life for the last twenty-nine days. It may seem too early to celebrate with one day to go, but being able to celebrate is a skill and I want you to make sure you know how to do it.

Celebration means to me:

How do you celebrate the big moments of life as well as the small? Marriage, graduations, and birthdays are all events that are predictable celebrations to cherish, but what about the times that aren't marked by a calendar? What about living a life of daily celebrations? What about celebrating all you have done for the past twenty-nine days?

If I could celebrate any way I wanted, I would:

Celebrating the process of living gives us the gift of personal satisfaction where true accomplishment resides. It is where we find the inner peace we crave, leaving our fear behind. It is not about the predictable times where we stop and do the obligatory pose for the camera. It is much larger than that.

Daily celebrations are valuable moments we create or discover that keep us in touch with what matters to us. I celebrate daily when I drink my favorite tea out of my favorite cup that reads LIFE IS GOOD. It reminds me to savor the moments.

List five celebrations you could turn into daily events:

1.
2.
3.
4.
5.

My most memorable events are when the spontaneity of life dictated my actions. Like the time my ex-husband and I stopped at a yard sale while we were driving through rural Wisconsin or when my nieces and nephews said their prayers during a family vacation in Upper Michigan or when I hopped on a plane to visit someone I loved because of a last-minute Internet special. Those are the times I relish and yearned to re-create. Yet, as we all know, re-creating a moment is impossible.

I tried for years to re-create the New Year's Eve I had when I was twenty-two. Each year I planned every detail of those evenings so I would avoid being disappointed. But I always was. So I judged those failed attempts as proving once again that I was in some way not good enough. Sure, I had some nice New Year's Eves after that, as well as great birthdays, but they paled in comparison to that special night long ago.

And that was the problem. I compared. Comparing our present life to a magical moment in the past is the death of living a life of celebration. Celebration is an attitude, a state of mind, a way of being. It cannot exist in the rules, boundaries, and expectations governed by fear.

So how does one celebrate life daily? It is being willing to see the good in all things. It is being willing to be happy even though everything isn't perfect in your world. It is seeing all you do through eyes of wonder. It is being open to miracles and magic happening each and every day. Living in gratitude for all there is regardless of your present circumstances. Being willing to see any opportunity as a time to celebrate life. Anticipating that all is well.

When was the last time you noticed the flowers blooming on the side of the freeway or the wind howling through the trees or the sound of birds chirping or laughter or the bank teller's smile or the kindness of a stranger? If it seems like ages ago, what is so fearful about the present that you need to live in the past or the future?

Or when was the last time you felt alive? I mean, really alive!

Filled with hope and promise and excitement and confidence while seeing each moment as wonderful and magnificent. Feeling alive is a sure sign you are celebrating life. Because celebration isn't about events, it is about loving the moment for being just that: a moment where you are fully alive. And feeling fully alive is an indication that you are truly living fearlessly.

Learning to experience heaven on earth will inspire you to live life to its fullest and appreciate the moments of joy that you experience, no matter how brief. As we move toward our last day together, enjoy today as if it was the only day that mattered.

Today, Heaven

Congratulations on reaching Day Twenty-nine. You have reached a milestone in transforming your life. Being true to yourself is getting easy, so now it is time to push it up a notch.

Please write a letter of commitment to yourself. Use the sample above as a guide. Think of what would make you feel better about yourself when you are having a bad day or when things are good and you are afraid it will end. How do you stay inspired and in action? Write some things you can do in your commitment letter. It may take a couple of drafts to be as concise and clear as you'd like. That's fine. If you need extra space, please grab your journal and continue writing. Get it all down on paper and then refine. Do not edit as you go—when you do, you are putting perfection over content. Content is what matters here.

Today, I commit to:

Please answer the following questions. Do not think about your answers.

When I was writing my letter of commitment, I felt ___
_____.

If I could manifest all I wrote down, my life would be

_____.

I am scared I would be able to _____.
This letter was easy because _____.
This letter was hard for me because _____.

Commitment is a fundamental step and one that you will refine for the rest of your life. I encourage you to write a commitment letter at least once a year. It will help you put your life into perspective.

Day 30

Let Me Introduce You
to Yourself

We started this sacred journey thirty days ago. You were
nervous, perhaps disbelieving, that you could make such a
radical change. But you persisted because you knew that
no other journey in your life is as important as living the life you are
supposed to live.

This is a day to celebrate. You started to change your life by giving credit where credit is due and acknowledging that changing your
life has to start first and foremost with yourself. You can have support, and you need support, from others, but real change comes from
within.

Now that you have reached Day Thirty, you need to know the truth
about this book: This is not the end of the journey. Much as life does
not have a finish line other than death, this journey does not end.

Imagine you are waking up in the morning one year from today.
Take a minute and describe your true self. What will you be wearing?
How is your day planned? What are you eating for breakfast? How do
you express your passion? Are you in a relationship? Be as detailed
and as specific as possible. What are your feelings, behaviors, and activities?

As you were describing yourself one year from today, how did it feel
to be you? Was it an honor? Scary? Empowering? Did you doubt your
ability to get there? Were you getting excited to live your true life?

What would it take for you to get there from here? You have already
made some amazing shifts in your life, so what's missing? What have
you yet to master? What would you have to change in your life for you
to become more true to who you are? Or even be willing to find that

out? What skills would you need to acquire? What qualities about yourself would you like to keep? Let go of? What must be forgiven?

It wasn't until I was thirty-four years old that I knew I had to learn to accept myself for who I was if I was ever going to become who I was meant to be. Before then I didn't want to accept myself. I didn't like who I was and I was convinced that if I accepted myself, all my motivation to change would be lost. I thought it meant accepting my imperfections as facts. I felt like giving up. If I had to accept myself the way I was, what was the point of trying to be better?

As we have gone through this journey together, I know you have discovered that finding your true self isn't about becoming perfect or knowing yourself inside out or knowing exactly what you want. Finding your true self is, in essence, a journey of self-acceptance. Of knowing who you are and knowing your perception can change at any minute. Giving yourself a break, and loving yourself as is, is one of the most important messages of this book. It includes learning that you have no weaknesses, only quirks, no imperfections, only unique qualities.

During the last thirty days you have learned that when you feel guilt or shame, you need to replace it with compassion and forgiveness. When you feel judged, replace it with understanding. When you feel left out, replace it with reaching out. When you feel scared, replace it with self-love. When you are not happy with any aspect of your life, it's just a call to accept yourself more fully. I don't mean quit growing. I do mean love no matter what.

Becoming true to your best self takes courage, because each day you must be willing to be wrong about everything to feel right about you for the rest of your life. Each day you must be willing to give up all you know to find out more of what you don't. It is exhilarating, scary, and enlightening.

And that is what I have come to know, and have shared with you how to achieve, throughout the last thirty days. I know that as soon as I was willing to accept myself as is, I quit judging. I quit trying to be perfect. I quit trying to please everyone. I quit trying to be a winner. Instead, I began to embrace my humanity. And my true self emerged fearlessly.

The first step in living a life that you are proud to call your own is learning to embrace your humanity. On Day One I asked you some important questions. Let's revisit them:

1. Are you willing to put personal integrity above a promise to another?
2. Are you willing to listen to your heart while using your head?
3. Are you willing to quit lying to yourself in order to start loving yourself?
4. Are you willing to be authentic even if it means being vulnerable?
5. Are you willing to invest in the life you have to get the life you want?

When you are able to say a resounding yes to each of those questions, you know you are being true to yourself. Throughout the last thirty days you have gained many skills that should help you say yes with conviction. Are you saying yes?

As we've discovered, the journey to your true self is a life filled with risk. You must risk if you want to live a life that you would be proud to call your own. Remember, fear thrives on safety. Love thrives on risk. As you risk, you are learning to love yourself as well as opening your heart to others. You are learning to be comfortable being uncomfortable. You are practicing being fearless.

Go ahead and list three risks you have taken in the past thirty days that prove you are fearless. If you need help, refer to the five questions above. If you are practicing or contemplating any of them, you were taking a risk.

1.
2.
3.

The journey to finding your true self takes a commitment to keep going no matter what. Keep going despite your feelings. Keep taking actions despite your fears. Keep focusing on your journey, the process. If you do, the results will take care of themselves. One of the critical factors of your journey is your ability to trust the process. Trusting the process includes trusting yourself.

Have you learned to trust yourself more than you did before? Do you trust that you know the difference between your empowering intuitive guidance system versus the disempowering voice of fear?

Are you willing to risk everything to follow your heart? Can you be sure you are doing what you must because you are guided rather than out of guilt?

Answering yes means you have truly changed your life in thirty days. Anyone can do it if they are willing to do the hard work necessary to make the changes that count. Changing your hair is one thing, changing your life is another.

List three changes you have made in the last thirty days:

1.
2.
3.

How do you feel about yourself now that you have made those changes?

List three changes you are still working on:

1.
2.
3.

List three changes you would like to make but haven't yet:

1.
2.
3.

If you made all of the changes above, how would your life be different?

Let's review what you have learned. Each day was devoted to sharing with you the tools that would shift your thoughts, feelings, and actions in a profound day. I wanted to give you a way to interface with the world that was empowering. Whether it is for yourself and your thoughts or being with another, the skills you have developed are useful in any type of situation.

Below is a list of the themes that were the focus for each day. Refer to this list as you go forward. If you feel unsure in a certain area, reread the chapter and rededicate yourself to finding the truth at its core.

Day 1: Courage
Day 2: Acknowledgment
Day 3: Confidence
Day 4: Passion
Day 5: Intention
Day 6: Risk
Day 7: Truth
Day 8: Discipline
Day 9: Shine
Day 10: Integrate
Day 11: Regrets
Day 12: Assertive
Day 13: Focus
Day 14: Lying
Day 15: Trust
Day 16: Balance
Day 17: Excuses
Day 18: Intuition
Day 19: Forgiveness
Day 20: Momentum
Day 21: Choice
Day 22: Humanity
Day 23: Gratitude
Day 24: Love
Day 25: Commitment
Day 26: Clarify
Day 27: Who Am I?

Day 28: Beauty
Day 29: Enjoyment
Day 30: The New You

You have learned many important skills over the last thirty days. You have faced your fears and conquered some demons. You have been willing to be wrong about everything you know to have a better life. And that is courageous. Learning who you are and being true to who you are is the most important journey you will ever take.

Be open to new opportunities that come your way. Get ready to be a truer and better you. And remember, stay fearless!

Gratitudes

Today, I am grateful for:

Brian Tart, editorial director of Dutton. Thank you for believing in me. Anna Cowles, editorial assistant, a gem. And Carole Baron, president of Dutton, a supportive spirit in my life. I am grateful for your continuous commitment to my work.

Amy Williams, my literary agent and Helen Shabason, my television agent: a winning combination of woman power! I admire your courage, tenacity, and beauty.

The entire staff at Dutton, THANK YOU! Thank you for all you do! Lisa Johnson, Kathleen Matthews, Bob Wojciechowski, Erin Sinesky, Robert Kempe, Liz Perl, Beth Mellow, and the entire *Change Your Life* PR team. As always, you bring out the best in me.

The entire staff at Hodder Headline in the United Kingdom and Australia. Rowena Webb, Kerry Hood, Lisa Highton, Ineke Hogendijk, Heidi Murphy, Ella Shanahan, Jaki Arthur, Natalie Coakes, and the entire Hodder Headline team. Thank you!

Mary-Ellis Bunim and Jon Murray, the creators of *Starting Over*. Thank you for giving me the opportunity to do what I do best—change lives. It is an honor to impact millions of people daily. I look forward to many more collaborations together. To the entire staff at Bunim-Murray Productions, including Bonnie, Sasha, Sarah, Damion,

Shannon, Jason, Gil and every single person who has contributed to *Starting Over.* And to Beck Media—Todd and Daniella—for your continuous media efforts.

Ed Wilson and the syndication team at NBC Enterprise for *Starting Over.* I am grateful for your commitment to change lives through the medium of television.

The Chicago *Starting Over* crew who put it all together. I am thankful for the leaders of the team: Jim Johnston, Linda Midgett, and Cliff Grant. I am especially grateful for the hard work displayed time and time again by the camera and sound crews, producers, associate producers, production assistants, and office staff. You make my job easy.

The creators of *Help Me Rhonda,* Talkback Productions, and Channel 5 in the United Kingdom. Special thanks goes to Claire Masters, my series producer, along with Paul Franklin, head honcho. And of course, Kerry Scourfield, who makes me look good. Double thanks goes to Kim Peat, commissioning editor at Channel 5, and Daisy Goodwin, executive producer at Talkback Productions. And to all the staff that creates, produces, edits, and promotes *Help Me Rhonda* . . . Thank you!

The Fearless Living Institute staff: Beth Karish, head goddess, DD Lerner, administrative assistant, and Cindee Ball, volunteer extraordinaire. You hold down the fort and keep it together while I do what I do. Never forget: You make a difference to me. And I am eternally grateful to you for giving so much of yourself and loving what you do. Thank you!

The Fearless Living Institute (FLI) core team: Michele Moore, Lura Fischer, Susie Peterson, Jerilyn Thiel, Janet Tingwald, and Cindy Tvinnereim. You are the heart of the Fearless Living Institute. Stanley Otterstrom, Martin Wenger, and Donlyn Whissen for your commitment to Get a Coach and FLI Ambassador programs. Rosie Laughlin, Bill Grout, Cindee Ball, Susan Kiefert, and Wendy Perkins for your contributions to facilitating growth in Become a Coach Program. And to all the Certified Fearless Living Coaches (CFLC) around the world for their commitment to spread the Fearless Word.

My friends who have kept me sane, my sisters, Cindy and Linda, and their respective families, who love me as I am. There is nothing else to say, only thank you!

My parents. That moment changed my life. I am proud to be called your daughter.

The viewers of *Starting Over* in the United States and *Help Me Rhonda* in the United Kingdom. To all the readers of my books, radio listeners, workshop participants, and Fearbuster Group leaders. To anyone who strives to be Fearless. I am grateful for our journey together. With your help, may the world become Fearless! Gxo

Ready to become Fearless . . .

Work with a Certified Fearless Living Coach?
Attend a Fearless Foundation Workshop?
Lead or join a Fearbuster Group?
Want to become a Life Coach?

To find out more about workshops and teleclasses, available private life coaches trained by Rhonda, all the ins and outs of starting your own Fearbuster Group, opportunities to meet Rhonda in person, and the latest happenings . . .

Visit Rhonda's website at www.fearlessliving.org.

Want to learn at your own pace, on your own schedule?

Become a paid member of the Fearless Living Institute (FLI) website and receive access to hundreds of hours of Rhonda sharing what she knows through audio clips and videos. You will be able to learn in the comfort of your home on-demand.

Visit Rhonda's website at www.fearlessliving.org.

Become a Certified Fearless Living Coach . . .

The Fearless Living Institite (FLI) has the most thorough, comprehensive, and business-building coaching training program in the world. It is the only coaching program that requires you to complete four prerequisites to help you find out if becoming a coach is really for you, saving you money and time. For more information, log on to www.fearlessliving.org to find out more.

Would you like your business to be more Fearless . . .

The Fearless Living Institute (FLI) is the gold standard for human potential in the business world! Benefits to our programs designed specifically for you are higher retention through increased employee and client satisfaction; increased staff productivity; maximum bottom-line efficiency; and a renewed ability to tap into the creativity and ingenuity of your employees. Contact the Fearless Living Institute at (303) 447-2704.

About the Author

Rhonda Britten, named America's favorite Life Coach, is the founder of the Fearless Living Institute. As the life coach on the Emmy Award–winning daytime reality drama, *Starting Over*, she has been called its, "Most Valuable Player" by the *New York Times*.

Rhonda has written several national bestsellers based on her fearless principles, including *Fearless Loving* and *Fearless Living* (translated into twelve languages). Her newest book is *Do I Look Fat In This?*

As a speaker, she shares with corporations her message of personal accountability while giving them practical, hands-on tools that make a bottom-line difference. Corporate clients have included Southwest Airlines, Northrup Grumman, and Blue Shield.

For more information on Rhonda, visit www.fearlessliving.org.